Happiness Becomes You

NOURISHING YOUR SOUL

Revitalize Your Being With Everything Around You

KURT DOYLE

Table of Contents

Chapter 1: How To Find Inner Peace And Happiness – 10 Things You Can Start Doing Today.. 6

Chapter 2: It's Okay To Feel Uncertain 12

Chapter 3: Happy People Create Time to Do What They Love Every Day.. 15

Chapter 4: It's Not Your Job to Tell Yourself "No" 18

Chapter 5: Happy People are Okay with Not Being Okay 21

Chapter 6: How To Use Affirmations For Success 23

Chapter 7: 8 Ways to Discover What's holding You Back From Achieving Your Visions 25

Chapter 8: How To Stop Feeling Overwhelmed 29

Chapter 9: Happy People Are Busy but Not Rushed.............................. 31

Chapter 10: 8 Ways To Deal With Setbacks In Life.................................. 33

Chapter 11: Believe in Yourself 39

Chapter 12: 8 Ways To Adopt New Thoughts That Will Be Beneficial To Your Life 41

Chapter 13: 8 Steps To Develop Beliefs That Will Drive you To Success 45

Chapter 14: How To Set Smart Goals 50

Chapter 15: Happy People Consciously Nurture A Growth Mindset .. 53

Chapter 16: Consistency Can Bring You Happiness 56

Chapter 17: 10 Habits of Muhammad Ali 61

Chapter 18: Happy People Don't Make Excuses 65

Chapter 19: Becoming High Achievers 67

Chapter 20: *8 Ways On How To Start Taking Actions* 72

Chapter 21: Happy People Create Time to Do What They Love Every Day.. 77

Chapter 22: Happy People Are Proactive About Relationships 80

Chapter 23: If You Commit to Nothing, You'll Be Distracted By Everything 83

Chapter 24: How to Eat With Mood in Mind 86

Chapter 25: How To Crush Your Goals This Quarter 89

Chapter 26: Happy People Choose to Exercise 92

Chapter 27: 10 Habits of Cristiano Ronaldo... 94

Chapter 28: 10 Habits of Jack Ma... 99

Chapter 29: Happy People Celebrate Other People's Success............ 103

Chapter 30: Become A High Performer... 105

Chapter 31: 7 Ways Your Behaviors Are Holding You Back 109

Chapter 32: Happy People Are Optimistic 114

Chapter 33: **10 Habits of Prophet Muhammad**....................................... 117

Chapter 34: 10 Reasons Money Can't Buy You Happiness 122

Chapter 1:
How To Find Inner Peace And Happiness – 10 Things You Can Start Doing Today

Today's life is increasingly hectic and unorganized. We're running a race to accomplish more. And this race to nowhere has brought increased stress, anxiety, and even depression for some of us. In the process we have lost peace, harmony, and organization in our lives. That's the reason many among us have turned around in search of inner peace.

We must be mindful that inner peace is not something that we can just simply switch on when we decide we need it.

Inner peace is a state of mind that more often than not requires a lifelong journey of self-discovery and soul-searching. It is worthwhile to keep working towards finding and attaining that restful peace of mind, heart, and soul that we all deserve in our lives.

So the question here arises is, "What is inner peace, and how one can find it?"

Achieving Inner peace and happiness is possible, and you don't need to meditate on top of a mountain to break the barrier to find peace inside you.

If you want to achieve inner peace, here are 10 things you can start right now in your life.

1. Carve out some time for yourself

Take time out of your busy schedule and just be alone with yourself. Instead of constantly seeking happiness externally, look inwards to find serenity. Instead of trying to derive happiness from your friends or physical things, really discover how you can be happy without external influences. Can you be happy simply being alone with your thoughts and desires? Can you strive to achieve a calm state of mind that is free of worries and problems? Or is there something you know you need to do but have been putting off for quite some time? Only when you look inwards can you discover more about what truly matters to you.

2. Set Boundaries.

If you are feeling overwhelmed and exhausted, it is because you are doing things that are actually causing you to feel more anxious and stressed out. Consider setting boundaries to your bad habits, procrastinations, addictions, and even to technology such as your phone time and social media. It is truly time to stop doing the unnecessary things that don't move the needle forward for us and to start making time for important things in your life.Spending time with people who don't really care about your well-being or growth is something that we also need to be mindful of. Set a limit on the time we engage in those relationship and instead make more room for yourself to look inwards.

3. Find Your Relaxation Mojo

Everyone has their own unique relaxation mojo – For some it is to exercise, for some it is to read, and for others spending time family or listening to music helps calms them down. You know exactly what makes you tick. After you have identified what that is, simply make time to do more of it in the day or week. The goal is to release any tension you may have and to recharge your engines for what lies ahead.

4. Avoid turning molehills into mountains.

This is something that many of us might struggle with. We take a small problem and turn it into a giant mammoth task, causing us to lose our stability in the process while also creating unwanted stress in our lives. We will never find peace and happiness if we amplify every small little issue that may rise up. Instead work on breaking these things down even further to make them manageable and fun to do.

5. Keep an eye on your emotions

It is easy to let our emotions rule our actions. If we are not mindful of how we manage the stressors that life will throw at us from day to day, we may end up becoming bitter people by the end of it all. Always find a way to release these negative emotions in a way that works for you. Allow space for positive energy to fill up those spaces after you've successfully detoxed yourself. If something is simply too overwhelming and it is causing you to be angry, stressed, anxious, and even burnt out, consider take a break from it completely and coming back to it once you have a clearer head and mind.

6. Unclutter your world, unclutter your mind.

Clutter is what causes confusion and chaos in our lives. Physical clutter from overwhelming amounts of stuff in your room, home, and workspace will also cause mental clutter in your mind. A tidy, uncluttered, and neat space is to best way to bring clarity to your thoughts. Sometimes we let our mind be filled with junk as well. From unhealthy thought patterns to ruminations of the past, we need to purge these from our system in order to truly find peace and happiness. Take the time to sort these out in all areas if your life. Your body and mind will greatly appreciate the effort.

7. Adopt a Minimalistic approach

You don't need a castle to live in, 100 dishes on your dining table, and a gigantic office to work.

One can live in a small apartment with a few rooms, eat simple food, and just have a table and chair for work. All you really need is a comfortable space where you can work and live smartly. A minimalistic approach towards life will bring peace of mind, reduce stress, and make the journey of achieving inner peace much easier for you.

8. Accept and let go.

One of the biggest hindrances between you and your search for inner peace is your reluctance to let go. Bad things happen to the best of us. Setbacks are inevitable. Instead of dwelling on your failures, celebrate your achievements instead. You are not the sum of your failures. Your failures are what makes you a better person. Don't hold yourself hostage for these feelings. Accept that setbacks are part of the game and simply look forward to the wonderful things that lie ahead.

9. Stop guessing.

Guessing and second guessing ourselves and others will never bring inner peace and happiness for us – it only serves to bring about uncertainty and hesitation. Instead of flipping a coin on every situation or decision, really dig deeper to find out whether something is truly what you want or need. Communicate these thoughts and feelings openly and honestly, it can save you from disappointment and misguided realities in the future.

10. Find The True Cause of Your Anxieties

Sometimes we waste our energy solving the wrong problems, and we go round and round searching for the reasons for our unhappiness. Ask yourself the right questions and find out what is really causing you pain. You may have subconsciously decided to bury it by hiding it under the carpet. It is always easier for us to escape and bury our heads in the sand when things get hard, but the pain will come back to haunt us eventually. Dig out these problems and anxieties and face them head on.

Bonus

Remember: There's always tomorrow

Sometimes life puts you on a harder path and you feel that this is not what you signed up for. But remember that there is always another day, another tomorrow. There is a season for everything and your time in the sun will come. Accept things as the way they are. Be patient and I firmly believe that good things will come to you.

Chapter 2:
It's Okay To Feel Uncertain

We are surrounded by a world that has endless possibilities. A world where no two incidents can predict the other. A realm where we are a slave to the unpredictable future and its repercussions.

Everyone has things weighing on their mind. Some of us know it and some of us keep carrying these weights unknowingly.

The uncertainty of life is the best gift that you never wanted. But when you come to realize the opportunities that lie at every uneven corner are worth living for.

Life changes fast, sometimes in our favor and sometimes not much. But life always has a way to balance things out. We only need to find the right approach to make things easier for us and the ones around us.

Everyone gets tested once in a while, but we need to find ways to cope with life when things get messy.

The worst thing the uncertainty of life can produce is the fear in your heart. The fear to never know what to expect next. But you can never let fear rule you.

To worry about the future ahead of us is pointless. So change the question from 'What if?' to 'What will I do if.'

If you already have this question popping up in your brain, this means that you are already getting the steam off.

You don't need to fear the uncertain because you can never wreck your life in any such direction from where there is no way back.

The uncertainty of life is always a transformation period to make you realize your true path. These uncertainties make you realize the faults you might have in your approach to things.

You don't need to worry about anything unpredictable and unexpected because not everything is out of your control every time. Things might not happen in a way you anticipated but that doesn't mean you cannot be prepared for it.

There are a lot of things that are in your control and you are well researched and well equipped to go around events. So use your experience to do the damage control.

Let's say you have a pandemic at your hand which you couldn't possibly predict, but that doesn't mean you cannot do anything to work on its effects. You can raise funds for the affected population. You can try to find new ways to minimize unemployment. You can find alternate ways to keep the economy running and so on.

Deal with your emotions as you cannot get carried away with such events being driven by your feelings.

Don't avoid your responsibilities and don't delay anything. You have to fulfill every task expected of you because you were destined to do it. The results are not predetermined on a slate but you can always hope for the best be the best version of yourself no matter how bad things get.

Life provides us with endless possibilities because when nothing is certain, anything is possible. So be your own limit.

Chapter 3:
Happy People Create Time to Do What They Love Every Day

Most of our days are filled with things that we need to do and the things we do to destress ourselves. But, in between all this, we never get time for things. We wanted to do things that bring us pure joy. So then the question is, When will we find time to do what we love? Then, when things calm down a bit and when the people who visit us leave or finish all the trips we have planned and wrap up our busy projects, and the kids will be grown, we will retire? Then, probably after we are dead, we will have more time.

You do not have to wait for things to get less busy or calmer. There will always be something coming up; trips, chores, visitors, errands, holidays, projects, death and illness. There is never going to be more time. Whatever you have been stuck in the past few years, it will always be like that. So now the challenge is not waiting for things to change it is to make time for things you love no matter how busy your life is. Sit down and think about what you want to do, something that you have been putting off. What is something that makes you feel fulfilled and happy? Everyone has those few things that make them fall in love with life think of what is that for you. If you haven't figured it out yet, we will give you some examples, and maybe you can try some of these things and see how that makes you feel.

- Communing with nature

- Going for a beautiful walk

- Creating or growing a business or an organization

- Hiking, running, biking, rowing, climbing

- Meditating, journaling, doing yoga, reflecting

- Communing with loved ones

- Crafting, hogging, blogging, logging, vlogging
- Reading aloud to kids
- Reading aloud to kids

Did you remember something you enjoyed doing, but as the responsibilities kept increasing, you sidelined it. Well, this is your sign to start doing what you loved to take time out for that activity every day, even if it is for 30 minutes only. Carve that time out for yourself, do it now. Once you start doing this, you will realize that you will have more energy because your brain will release serotonin, and your energy level will increase. Secondly, your confidence will improve because you will be making something love every day, and that will constantly help you gain confidence because you will be putting yourself in a happy, self-loving state. You will notice that you have started enjoying life more when you do something you love once a day. It makes the rest of your day brighter and happier. You will also want to constantly continue learning and growing because your brain will strive to do more and more of the thing you like to do, and that will eventually lead to an increased desire of learning and growing. Lastly, your motivation will soar because you will have something to look forward to that brings you pure joy.

Chapter 4:
It's Not Your Job to Tell Yourself "No"

How many times have you had the chance to go around something that could have changed your life? What were your thoughts when you decided to enter a state where even the slightest thought of failure leads you to stop acting on it?

I'm sure every one of us has a good reason behind everything we opt to do or don't in our lives.

But there is never a good enough reason to back down just because we have some examples of failures on our hands.

No one can decide what reality and nature have decided for them. Everyone must learn to juggle life and play with every piece they get a hand on.

Everything in life is meant to be taken as a risk. You can never learn to swim till you get your first dive in a deep pool. You never learn to ride a bike till you have no one behind you to stop you from falling.

Everyone needs a bump every now and then. And when you finally decide to hike that hurdle, you finally start to see the horizon.

We all seem to get depressed more easily than we start to get motivated. We seem to get carried away with every stone that life throws back at us but we never try to catch that stone. We never try to indulge in one more suffering just to get better at what we are tested with.

Nobody wants to fail and that's why no one wants to take a chance at what might fail.

The mere fear of facing failure makes us build a mechanism of self-defense that forces us to say 'No' to anything that might hurt us one day.

But the reality is that it is illogical to stop just so you are afraid to face the reality. The reality is that you are a sane human and this is life. Life tests us in ways hardly imaginable.

When you say 'No' to yourself, it rarely means 'Not Now'. It always means 'Maybe some other time'. But deep down we already know that we will never attempt to do that thing. At least not consciously.

We always try for the best. We try to be the best at what we already have and are already doing. We are motivated enough to try new things, things that are more scary and unknown to us.

What we really should be doing is to try and get a taste of newer victories. Trying to search for new horizons. Trying to get what most fail to achieve. Because every other man or woman is just like us, afraid to fail and avoiding embarrassment. Our embarrassments are mostly self-imposed and we are the better judge of our failures.

There is no motivation and inspiration more powerful in the world than the spark that ignites within you.

Our sole purpose in life is to embrace everything that we come across. It is never to prevent something just because you don't have the courage to face your failures yet.

Chapter 5:
Happy People are Okay with Not Being Okay

All of us have a tendency where we constantly try to make people feel better about ourselves. We are fundamentally driven by empathy and compassion but what happens often is that these two are misdirected. Then we put our idea of okay onto other people and ourselves. Have you ever wondered what would it feel like when we simply whatever comes our way? When we are physically sick, of course, we take medicines to feel better, but there are also times when we are in emotional pain, and then we have no medicine to take and what happens is we seek out a solution, and that puts off the process where we can feel our feelings.

If you go through a breakup and do not allow yourself to feel the pain, what you will do is harm the next person you will date or sabotage your relationship with them. What will heal your wound is actively processing your emotions. This is not at all going to be comfortable, but it is essential for your emotional growth. What you need to do is start shedding the shame that surrounds not being okay. Just because you are in pain and not at the top of your work does not mean that you are weak. You also need to know that you are not the only one who thinks like that. We have been conditioned in this way of dysfunctional thinking and feeling. Most of us think that this is normal and normal is fine, but if you talk about health, that is a different story.

Of course, there are actions that you take that help you release the emotional pain you are in, but you have to remember that almost all of these actions will ask you to focus on yourself before you start focusing on others—for example, yoga. Yoga teaches you that your pain is not permanent, and it also tells us about how we have to be in an uncomfortable pose for a while to release that pain.

You have to remember that the only focus over here is you and you alone, but because we are all on a journey, we do get wind up in others' problems, which helps us find profound connections with them. It is okay to feel scared, or to feel pain, to feel uncertain, to feel lonely, to feel grief, it is okay to not be okay, and these are some of the things that you should never forget.

All the pain that you are feeling right now is not permanent. It will eventually pass. What you can do is honour your emotional experience by not avoiding it and being present for it; you should not try to distract yourself with every fibre of your being. This is a process that will help you heal and grow and move forward on this road. Show up for whatever you feel, even if it is just for a day.

Chapter 6:
How To Use Affirmations For Success

Affirmations are best described as a self-help strategy that is used to promote self-confidence and belief in your abilities. There might come a million instances where you felt like you needed to affirm yourself, and there would be many moments when you have probably affirmed yourself without even realizing it. Simple sentences like "I've got what it takes" or "I believe in my ability to succeed" shift your focus away from the perceived inadequacies or failures and direct your focus towards your strengths. While affirmations may not be a magic bullet for instant success, they generally work as a tool for shifting your mindset and achieving your goals.

Neuroplasticity, or our brain's ability to adapt and change to different circumstances throughout our lives, makes us understand what makes affirmations work and how to make them more effective. Creating a mental image beforehand of doing something that you're scared of, like acing a nerve-wracking interview or bungee jumping to conquer your fear of heights, can encourage your brain to take these positive affirmations as fact, and soon your actions will tend to follow.

Repeating affirmations can help you boost your confidence and motivation, but you still must take some action yourself. Affirmations are a step towards the change, not the change itself. They can also help you to achieve your goals by strengthening your confidence by reminding you that you're in control of your success and what you can do right now to achieve it. Affirmations give you a list of long-standing patterns and beliefs, and it makes you act as if you've already succeeded. Understand that affirmations alone can't produce a change in every situation. You have to take some actions too along with them. Similarly, affirming your traits can also help you see yourself in a new light.

To get the most benefits from affirmations, start a regular practice and make it a habit. Say affirmations upon waking up and getting into bed; give them at least 3-5 minutes. Repeat each of your affirmations ten times, focus on the words that leave your mouth. Believe them to be true while saying them. Make it a consistent habit. You have to be patient and stick with your practice, and it might take some time before you see evident changes. Practicing affirmations can also activate the reward system in your brain, which can impact how you experience both emotional and physical pain. The moment you start managing your stress and other life difficulties, it would help you promote faith in yourself and boost self-empowerment.

Chapter 7:
8 Ways to Discover What's holding You Back From Achieving Your Visions

We all have dreams, and I have no questions; you have made attempts at seeking after your goals. Oh, as a general rule, life's battles get the better of you and keep you down. The pressure of everyday life, again and again, puts you down. Regardless of your determination, devotion, and want, alone, they are not enough.

Being here exhibits you are not able to settle for a mediocre life and hidden desires. To help you in your goal of seeking after your objectives, you must become acquainted with those things keeping you down. When you do, you will want to eliminate every single reason keeping you down.

1. Fear

The deep-rooted foe is very likely a critical factor in keeping many of you from seeking after your objectives. It prevents you from acting, making you scared of venturing out. Dread is the thing that keeps you down. Dread is one reason why we don't follow what we truly need throughout everyday life.

- Fear of disappointment
- Fear of dismissal
- Fear of mocking

- Fear of disappointment

Quit allowing your feelings of fear to keep you down!

2. Procrastination

Putting things off till the following week, one month from now, one year from now, and regularly forever. You're not exactly sure the thing you're hanging tight for, but rather when whatever it happens, you'll be prepared to start seeking after your objectives. Be that as it may, this day never comes. Your fantasy stays as just a fantasy. Putting things off can just keep you down.

Quit allowing your Procrastination to keep you down!

3. Justifications

Do you find yourself procrastinating and making excuses for why you can't start working toward your goals? Those that succeed in accomplishing their objectives can overcome obstacles. So many individuals make excuses for themselves, believing they can't achieve a better career, start their own business, or find their ideal lifemate.

- It isn't the correct time
- I am insufficient
- I am too old/young

Don't allow your excuses to hold you back any longer!

4. Lack of Confidence

Lack of confidence in yourself or your ability to achieve your goals will inevitably hold you back. Our actions, or lack thereof, are influenced by what goes on in our subconscious mind. We have self-limiting and negative beliefs that may be preventing us from enjoying an extraordinary life.

Nothing will be able to stop you if you believe in yourself. Bringing your limiting beliefs into focus will help you achieve your objectives.

Don't let your lack of confidence keep you back!

5. There Isn't A Big Picture

Others refer to what I call a breakthrough goal as a BHAG - Big Hairy Audacious Goal. A goal is what you need to keep you motivated and drive you to achieve it every day. Start small and dream big. You'll need a strong enough passion to propel you forward. Your ambitions will not motivate you until you first dream big.

For your objectives to be beneficial to you, they must assist you in realizing your ambitions. Those lofty ambitions. Goals can only motivate you, help you stay focused, and help you make the adjustments you need to make, as well as provide you the fortitude to overcome difficulties as you chase your big-picture dreams if they matter to you.

Stop allowing your big picture to stifle your progress!

6. Inability To Concentrate

Your chances of success are slashed every moment you lose focus. When we spread our focus too thin, we dilute our effort and lose the ability to focus on the most significant tasks. When you're pulled in a lot of different directions and have a lot of conflicting priorities fighting for your attention, it's easy to lose track of what's important. Any attempts to achieve vital goals will be harmed as a result of this.

Stop allowing your lack of concentration to keep you back!

7. Failure to Make a Plan

Finally, if you don't have a strategy, it's easy to become lost along the route. Consider driving across the country without a map, say from London to Glasgow. While you have a rough route in mind, there are many lands to cover and a lot of false turns and dead ends to be avoided. You can get there with the help of a GPS. It plots your path and creates a plan for you. A plan provides you with the road map you need to reach your objectives. This is the process of determining what you need to accomplish to reach your objectives. This is where you put in the time and effort to write out a plan of the steps you need to follow, the resources you'll need, and the amount of time you'll need to invest.

Stop allowing the lack of a strategy holds you back!

8. Not Keeping Track of Your Progress and Making Necessary Modifications

Goals, by their very nature, take time to attain. Therefore it's critical to keep track of your progress. You won't know what's working and what's not if you don't get quick and actionable feedback. You won't be able to tell when to alter or when to keep doing what you're doing. Anyone who is continuously successful in accomplishing their goals also reviews their goals and progress regularly. Regularly reviewing your goals allows you to make early modifications to stay on track.

Stop allowing not reviewing and adjusting your progress to hold you back!

Chapter 8:
How To Stop Feeling Overwhelmed

There might come a million instances in your life when you will feel overwhelmed. Whether it's college, work, social obligations, family, or life in general, life can get anxious, stressed, and overwhelmed at certain times. It's important to recognize these feelings and give yourself grace when you have these feelings. Try to dive deeper into your emotions and understand what's causing them, don't brush them off or push through whatever's causing you to feel anxious. Your mental health matters more than anything, and if you're feeling the squeeze, know that you can always take a step back.

When things start to feel a little too much for you, take a deep breath and step away. If you feel anxious or overwhelmed, start doing some breathing exercises to alleviate those feelings. If the thing that's causing you anxiety is right in front of you, take a step away from it and create some separation between you that's overwhelming you. Deep breathing exercises will promote relaxation and would lower your stress response immediately. Understand that we all go through these phases, and it's completely okay and normal to feel like this. Cut yourself some slack and be kind towards yourself. If you're unable to do that chore or have to ask for some extension in your deadline, then do that. Your mental health should be your top priority.

While most of the time, we might want to get isolated or want everyone to leave us alone in our times of stress and anxiety, it's better to reach out to a loved one and ask for their support and help. You can also virtually chat to an online psychologist and rant to them to feel better. Or you can pick up the phone and call your friends or family and ask for their comfort and consolation.

You can also find a hobby that you find relaxation in. It can either be swimming, driving, baking, reading, or any of the stuff that calms your mind and you enjoy doing it. Writing down your reasons for anxiousness and being overwhelmed can also be a great way to alleviate those feelings. It helps you express yourself freely and provides a sense of relief once all of those thoughts are out of your head. Always remember that whatever you're feeling is temporary. With the right coping mechanisms and support, you can always take care of yourself when things start to go south. Protect your time and space and create healthy boundaries for yourself.

Chapter 9:
Happy People Are Busy but Not Rushed

Dan Pink points to an interesting new research finding — the happiest people are those that are very busy but don't feel rushed:

Who among us are the happiest? Newly published research suggests that fortunate folks have little or no excess time and yet seldom feel rushed.

This clicks with me. I love blogging, but I hate being under time pressure to get it done. This tension is very nicely demonstrated in a recent study by Hsee et al. (2010). When given a choice, participants preferred to do nothing unless given the tiniest possible reason to do something: a piece of candy. Then they sprang into action.

Not only did people only need the smallest inducement to keep busy, but they were also happier when doing something rather than nothing. It's as if people understand that being busy will keep them happier, but they need an excuse of some kind.

Having plenty of time gives you a feeling of control. Anything that increases your *perception of control* over a situation (whether it increases your control or not) can substantially decrease your stress level.

In Colorado, Steve Maier at the University of Boulder says that the degree of control that organisms can exert over something that creates stress determines whether the stressor alters the organism's functioning. His findings indicate that only uncontrollable stressors cause harmful effects. Inescapable or uncontrollable stress can be destructive, whereas the same stress that feels escapable is less destructive, significantly so… **Over and over, scientists see that the perception of control over a stressor alters the stressor's impact.**

But heavy time pressure stresses you out and [kills creativity](). Low-to-moderate time pressure produces the best results.

If managers regularly set impossibly short time-frames or impossibly high workloads, employees become stressed, unhappy, and unmotivated—burned out. Yet, people hate being bored. It was rare for any participant in our study to report a day with very low time pressure, such days—when they did occur—were also not conducive to positive inner work life. In general, low-to-moderate time pressure seems optimal for sustaining positive thoughts, feelings, and drives.

Your reaction to being too busy and under time pressure might be to want to do nothing. But that can drop you into the bottom left corner. And this makes you [more unhappy than anything]():

…**surveys "continue to show the least happy group to be those who quite often have excess time." Boredom, it seems, is burdensome.**

So, stay busy—set goals. Challenge yourself, but make sure you have plenty of time to feel in control of the situation.

This is how games feel. And games are fun.

Chapter 10:
8 Ways To Deal With Setbacks In Life

Life is never the same for anyone - It is an ever-changing phenomenon, making you go through all sorts of highs and lows. And as good times are an intrinsic part of your life, so are bad times. One day you might find yourself indebted by 3-digit figures while having only $40 in your savings account. Next day, you might be vacationing in Hawaii because you got a job that you like and pays $100,000 a year. There's absolutely no certainty to life (except passing away) and that's the beauty of it. You never know what is in store for you. But you have to keep living to see it for yourself. Setbacks in life cannot be avoided by anyone. Life will give you hardships, troubles, break ups, diabetes, unpaid bills, stuck toilet and so much more. It's all a part of your life.

Here's 8 ways that you might want to take notes of, for whenever you may find yourself in a difficult position in dealing with setback in life.

1. **Accept and if possible, embrace it**

The difference between accepting and embracing is that when you accept something, you only believe it to be, whether you agree or disagree. But when you embrace something, you truly KNOW it to be true and accept it as a whole. There is no dilemma or disagreement after you have embraced something.

So, when you find yourself in a difficult situation in life, accept it for what it is and make yourself whole-heartedly believe that this problem in your life, at this specific time, is a part of your life. This problem is what makes you complete. This problem is meant for you and only you can go through it. And you will. Period. There can be no other way.

The sooner you embrace your problem, the sooner you can fix it. Trying to bypass it will only add upon your headaches.

2. Learn from it

Seriously, I can't emphasize how important it is to LEARN from the setbacks you face in your life. Every hardship is a learning opportunity. The more you face challenges, the more you grow. Your capabilities expand with every issue you solve—every difficulty you go through, you rediscover yourself. And when you finally deal off with it, you are reborn. You are a new person with more wisdom and experience.

When you fail at something, try to explore why you failed. Be open-minded about scrutinizing yourself. Why couldn't you overcome a certain situation? Why do you think of this scenario as a 'setback'? The moment you find the answers to these questions is the moment you will have found the solution.

3. Execute What You Have Learnt

The only next step from here is to execute that solution and make sure that the next time you face a similar situation, you'll deal with it by having both your arms tied back and blindfolded. All you have to do is remember what you did in a similar past experience and reapply your previous solution.

Thomas A. Edison, the inventor of the light bulb, failed 10,000 times before finally making it. And he said "I have not failed. I just found 10,000 ways that won't work".

The lesson here is that you have to take every setback as a lesson, that's it.

4. Without shadow, you can never appreciate light

This metaphor is applicable to all things opposite in this universe. Everything has a reciprocal; without one, the other cannot exist. Just as without shadow, we wouldn't have known what light is, similarly, without light, we could've never known about shadow. The two opposites identify and complete each other.

Too much of philosophy class, but to sum it up, your problems in life, ironically, is exactly why you can enjoy your life. For example, if you are a chess player, then defeating other chess players will give you enjoyment while getting defeated will give you distress. But, when you are a chess prodigy—you have defeated every single chess player on earth and there's no one else to defeat, then what will you do to derive pleasure? Truth is, you can now no longer enjoy chess. You have no one to defeat. No one gives you the fear of losing anymore and as a result, the taste of winning has lost its appeal to you.

So, whenever you face a problem in life, appreciate it because without it, you can't enjoy the state of not having a problem. Problems give you the pleasure of learning from them and solving them.

5. View Every Obstacle As an opportunity

This one's especially for long term hindrances to your regular life. The COVID-19 pandemic for instance, has set us back for almost two years now. As distressing it is, there is also some positive impact of it. A long-term setback opens up a plethora of new avenues for you to explore. You suddenly get a large amount of time to experiment with things that you have never tried before.

When you have to pause a regular part of your life, you can do other things in the meantime. I believe that every one of us has a specific talent and most people never know what their talent is simply because they have never tried that thing.

6. Don't Be Afraid to experiment

People pursue their whole life for a job that they don't like and most of them never ever get good at it. As a result, their true talent gets buried under their own efforts. Life just carries on with unfound potential. But when some obstacle comes up and frees you from the clutches of doing what you have been doing for a long time, then you should get around and experiment. Who knows? You, a bored high school teacher, might be a natural at tennis. You won't know it unless you are fired from that job and actually play tennis to get over it. So whenever life gives you lemons, quit trying to hold on to it. Move on and try new things instead.

7. Stop Comparing yourself to others

The thing is, we humans are emotional beings. We become emotionally vulnerable when we are going through something that isn't supposed to be. And in such times, when we see other people doing fantastic things in life, it naturally makes us succumb to more self-loathing. We think lowly of our own selves and it is perfectly normal to feel this way. Talking and comapring ourselves to people who are seemingly untouched by setbacks is a counterproductive move. You will listen to their success-stories and get depressed—lose self-esteem. Even if they try their best to advise you, it won't get through to you. You won't be able to relate to them.

8. Talk to people other people who are having their own setbacks in life

I'm not asking you to talk to just any people. I'm being very specific here: talk to people who are going through bad times as well.

If you start talking to others who are struggling in life, perhaps more so compared to you, then you'll see that everyone else is also having difficulties in life. It will seem natural to you. Moreover, having talked with others might even show you that you are actually doing better than all these other people. You can always find someone who is dealing with more trouble than you and that will enlighten you. That will encourage you. If someone else can deal with tougher setbacks in life, why can't you?

Besides, listening to other people will give you a completely new perspective that you can use for yourself if you ever find yourself in a similar situation as others whom you have talked with.

Conclusion

Setbacks are a part of life. Without them we wouldn't know what the good times are. Without them we wouldn't appreciate the success that we have gotten. Without them we wouldn't cherish the moments that got us to where we are heading to. And without them there wouldn't be any challenge to fill our souls with passion and fire. Take setbacks as a natural process in the journey. Use it to fuel your drive. Use it to move your life forward one step at a time.

Chapter 11:
Believe in Yourself

Listen up. I want to tell you a story. This story is about a boy. A boy who became a man, despite all odds. You see, when he was a child, he didn't have a lot going for him. The smallest and weakest in his class, he had to struggle every day just to keep up with his peers. Every minute of every hour was a fight against an opponent bigger and stronger than he was - and every day he was knocked down. Beaten. Defeated. But... despite that... despite everything that was going against him... this small, weak boy had one thing that separated him from hundreds of millions of people in this world. A differentiating factor that made a difference in the matter of what makes a winner in this world of losers. You see this boy believed in himself. No matter the odds, he believed fundamentally that he had the power to overcome anything that got in his way! It didn't matter how many times he was knocked down, he got RIGHT BACK UP!

Now it wasn't easy. It hurt like hell. Every time he failed was another reminder of how far behind he was. A reminder of the nearly insurmountable gap between him and everyone else and lurking behind that reminder was the temptation, the suggestion to just give up. Throw in the towel. Surrender the win. Yet believe me when I tell you that no matter HOW tough things got, no matter HOW much he wanted to give in, a small voice in his heart keep saying... not today... just once more... I know it hurts but I can try again... Just. Once. More.

You see more than anything in this world HE KNEW that deep inside him was a greatness just WAITING to be tapped into! A power that most people would never see, but not him. It didn't matter what the world threw at him, because he'd be damned if he let his potential die alongside him. And all it took? All it required to unlock the chasm of greatness inside was a moment to realise the lies the world tried to tell him. In less than a second he recognised the light inside that would ignite a spark of success to address the ones who didn't believe that he could do it. The ones who told him to give up! Get out! Go home and roam the streets where failure meets those who weren't born to sit at the seat at the top!

Yet what they didn't know is that being born weak didn't matter any longer 'cause in his fight to succeed he became stronger. Rising up to the heights beyond, he WOULD NOT GIVE UP till he forged a bond within his heart that ensured NO MATTER THE ODDS, no matter what anyone said about him, no matter what the world told him, he had something that NO ONE could take away from him. A power so strong it transformed this boy into a man. A loser into a winner. A failure into a success. That, is the power of self-belief...

Chapter 12:
8 Ways To Adopt New Thoughts That Will Be Beneficial To Your Life

"Each morning we are born again. What we do today is what matters most." - Buddha

Is your glass half-empty or half-full? Answering this age-old question may reflect your outlook on life, your attitude toward yourself, whether you're optimistic or pessimistic, or it may even affect your health. Studies show that personality traits such as optimism and pessimism play a considerable role in determining your health and well-being. The positive thinking that comes with optimism is a practical part of stress management. Positive thinking in no way means that we keep our heads in the sand and ignore life's less pleasant situations. Instead, you have to approach the unpleasantness more positively and productively. Always think that something best is going to happen, and ignore the worst-case scenarios.

Here are some ways for you to adopt new thoughts that will benefit your outlook on life.

1. Breaking Out Old Thinking Patterns

We all can get stuck in a loop of specific thoughts. Sure, they may look comfortable on the outside, but we don't realize that these thoughts are what's holding us back most of the time. It's crucial to let fresh ideas and thoughts into your life and break away from the negative ones to see new paths ahead. We could start by challenging our assumptions in every situation. We may already assume what's about to happen if we fall into some condition, but trying new preconceptions can open up some exciting possibilities for us.

2. Rephrase The Problem

Your creativity can get limited by how you define or frame your problems. If you keep on looking at the problem from one side only, chances are you won't get much exposure to the solution. Whereas, if you look at it in different ways and different angles, new solutions can emerge. For example, the founder of Uber, Garret Camp, could have focused on buying and managing enough vehicles for him to make a profit. Instead, he looked more into how he could best entertain the passengers and thus, made a powerful app for their comfort.

3. Think In Reverse

Try turning the problem upside-down if you're having difficulties finding a new approach. Flip the situation and explore the opposite of what you want to achieve. This can help you present innovative ways to tackle the real issue. If you're going to take a good picture, try all of its angles first so you can understand which grade will be more suitable and which angles you should avoid. If you want to develop a new design for your website, try its worst look first and then make it the exact opposite. Apply different types of creativity to tackle your problems.

4. **Make New Connections**

Another way to generate new ideas and beneficial thoughts is by making unique and unexpected connections. Some of the best ideas click to you by chance, you hear or see something utterly unconnected to the situation you're trying to solve, and an idea has occurred to you almost instantly. For instance, architect Mick Pearce developed a groundbreaking climate-control system by taking the concept from the self-cooling mounds built by termites. You can pick on any set of random words, picture prompts, and objects of interest and then look for the novel association between them and your problem.

5. **Finding Fresh Perspectives**

Adding extra dynamism to your thinking by taking a step back from your usual standpoint and viewing a problem through "fresh eyes" might be beneficial for you to tackle an issue and give new thoughts. You could also talk to someone with a different perspective, life experience, or cultural background and would be surprised to see their approach. Consider yourself being the other person and see life from their eyes, their point of view.

6. **Focus On The Good Things**

Challenges and struggles are a part of life. When you're faced with obstacles, try and focus on the good part, no matter how seemingly insignificant or small it seems. If you keep looking for it, you will definitely find the proverbial silver lining in every cloud if it's not evident in the beginning.

7. Practice Gratitude

Practicing gratitude is said to reduce stress, foster resilience, and improve self-esteem. If you're going through a bad time, think of people, moments, or things that bring you some kind of comfort and happiness and express your gratitude once in a while. This could be anything, from thanking your loved one to lending a helping hand to anyone.

8. Practice Positive Self-Talk

We sometimes are our own worst critics and tend to be the hardest on ourselves. This can cause you to form a negative opinion of yourself. This could be prevented by practicing positive self-talk. As a result, this could influence your ability to regulate your feelings, thoughts, and behaviors under stress.

Conclusion

Developing a positive attitude can help you in many ways than you might realize. When you practice positive thinking, you consciously or subconsciously don't allow your mind to entertain any negative thoughts. You will start noticing remarkable changes all around you. By reducing your self-limiting beliefs, you will effectively grow as you have never imagined before. You can change your entire outlook on life by harnessing the power of positive thinking. You will also notice a significant boost in your confidence.

Chapter 13:
8 Steps To Develop Beliefs That Will Drive you To Success

'Success' is a broad term. There is no universal definition of success, it varies from person to person considering their overall circumstances. We can all more or less agree that confidence plays a key role in it, and confidence comes from belief.

Even our most minute decisions and choices in life are a result of believing in some specific outcome that we have not observed yet.

However, merely believing in an ultimate success will not bring fortune knocking at your door. But, it certainly can get you started—take tiny steps that might lead you towards your goal. Now, since we agree that having faith can move you towards success, let's look at some ways to rewire your brain into adopting productive beliefs.

Here are 8 Steps to Develop Beliefs That Will Drive You To Success:

1. **Come Up With A Goal**

Before you start, you need to decide what you want to achieve first. Keep in mind that you don't have to come up with something very specific right away because your expectations and decisions might change over time. Just outline a crude sense of what 'Achievement' and 'Success' mean to you in the present moment.

Begin here. Begin now. Work towards getting there.

2. Put Your Imagination Into Top Gear

"Logic will take you from A to B. Imagination will take you everywhere", said Albert Einstein.

Imagination is really important in any scenario whatsoever. It is what makes us humans different from animals. It is what gives us a reason to move forward—it gives us hope. And from that hope, we develop the will to do things we have never done before.

After going through the first step of determining your goal, you must now imagine yourself being successful in the near future. You have to literally picture yourself in the future, enjoying your essence of fulfilment as vividly as you can. This way, your ultimate success will appear a lot closer and realistic.

3. Write Notes To Yourself

Writing down your thoughts on paper is an effective way to get those thoughts stuck in your head for a long time. This is why children are encouraged to write down what is written in the books instead of memorizing them just by reading. You have to write short, simple, motivating notes to yourself that will encourage you to take actions towards your success. It doesn't matter whether you write in a notebook, or on your phone or wherever—just write it. On top of that, occasionally read what you've written and thus, you will remain charged with motivation at all times.

4. Make Reading A Habit

There are countless books written by successful people just so that they can share the struggle and experience behind their greatest achievements. In such an abundance of manuscripts, you may easily find books that portray narratives similar to your life and circumstances. Get reading and expand your knowledge. You'll get never-thought-before ideas that will guide you through your path to success. Reading such books will tremendously strengthen your faith in yourself, and in your success. Read what other successful people believed in—what drove them. You might even find newer beliefs to hold on to. No wonder why books are called 'Man's best friend'.

5. Talk To People Who Motivates You

Before taking this step, you have to be very careful about who you talk to. Basically, you have to speak out your goals and ambitions in life to someone who will be extremely supportive of you. Just talk to them about what you want, share your beliefs and they will motivate you from time to time towards success. They will act as powerful reminders. Being social beings, no human can ever reject the gist of motivation coming from another human being—especially when that is someone whom you can rely on comfortably. Humans have been the sole supporter of each other since eternity.

6. Make A Mantra

Self-affirming one-liners like 'I can do it', 'Nothing can stop me', 'Success is mine' etc. will establish a sense of firm confidence in your subconscious mind. Experts have been speculative about the power of our subconscious mind for long. The extent of what it can do is still beyond our grasp. But nonetheless, reciting subtle mantras isn't a difficult task. Do it a couple of times every day and it will remain in your mind for ages, without you giving any conscious thought to it. Such subconscious affirmations may light you up in the right moment and show you the path to success when you least expect it.

7. Reward Yourself From Time To Time

Sometimes, your goals might be too far-fetched and as a result, you'll find it harder to believe in something so improbable right now. In a situation like this, what you can do is make short term objectives that ultimately lead to your main goal and for each of those objectives achieved, treat yourself with a reward of any sort—absolutely anything that pleases you. This way, your far cry success will become more apparent to you in the present time. Instant rewards like these will also keep you motivated and make you long for more. This will drive you to believe that you are getting there, you are getting closer and closer to success.

8. Having Faith In Yourself

Your faith is in your hands alone. How strongly you believe in what you deserve will motivate you. It will steer the way for self-confidence to fulfill your inner self. You may be extremely good at something but due to the lack of faith in your own capabilities, you never attempted it—how will you ever know that you were good at that? Your faith in yourself and your destined success will materialize before you through these rewards that you reserve for yourself. You absolutely deserve this!

Final Thoughts

That self-confidence and belief and yourself, in your capabilities and strengths will make you work towards your goal. Keep in mind that whatever you believe in is what you live for. At the end of the day, each of us believed in something that made us thrive, made us work and move forward. Some believed in the military, some believed in maths, some believed in thievery—everyone had a belief which gave them a purpose—the purpose of materializing their belief in this world. How strongly you hold onto your belief will decide how successful you will become.

Chapter 14:
How To Set Smart Goals

Setting your goals can be a tough choice. It's all about putting your priorities in such a way that you know what comes first for you. It's imperative to be goal-oriented to set positive goals for your present and future. You should be aware of your criteria for setting your goals. Make sure your plan is attainable in a proper time frame to get a good set of goals to be achieved in your time. You would need hard work and a good mindset for setting goals. Few components can help a person reach their destination. Control what you choose because it will eternally impact your life.

To set a goal to your priority, you need to know what exactly you want. In other words, be specific. Be specific in what matters to you and your goal. Make sure that you know your fair share of details about your idea, and then start working on it once you have set your mind to it. Get a clear vision of what your goal is. Get a clear idea of your objective. It is essential to give a specification to your plan to set it according to your needs.

Make sure you measure your goals. As in, calculate the profit or loss. Measure the risks you are taking and the benefits you can gain from them. In simple words, you need to quantify your goals to know what order to set them into. It makes you visualize the amount of time it will take or the energy to reach the finish line. That way, you can calculate your goals and their details. You need to set your mind on the positive technical growth of your goal. That is an essential step to take to put yourself to the next goal as soon as possible.

If you get your hopes high from the start, it may be possible that you will meet with disappointment along the way. So, it would be best if you made sure that your goals are realistic and achievable. Make sure your goal is within reach. That is the reality check you need to force in your mind that is your goal even attainable? Just make sure it is, and everything will go as planned. It doesn't mean to set small goals. There is a difference between big goals and unrealistic goals. Make sure to limit your romantic goals, or else you will never be satisfied with your achievement.

Be very serious when setting your goals, especially if they are long-term goals. They can impact your life in one way or another. It depends on you how you take it. Make sure your goals are relevant. So, that you can gain real benefit from your goals. Have your fair share of profits from your hard work and make it count. Always remember why the goal matters to you. Once you get the fundamental idea of why you need this goal to be achieved, you can look onto a bigger picture in the frame. If it doesn't feel relevant, then there is no reason for you to continue working for. Leave it as it is if it doesn't give you what you applied for because it will only drain your energy and won't give you a satisfactory outcome.

Time is an essential thing to keep in focus when working toward your goals. You don't want to keep working on one thing for too long or too short. So, keep a deadline. Keep a limit on when to work on your goal. If it's worth it, give it your good timer, but if not, then don't even waste a second on it. They are just some factors to set your goals for a better future. These visionary goals will help you get through most of the achievements you want to get done with.

Chapter 15:
Happy People Consciously Nurture A Growth Mindset

"Without continual growth and progress, such words as improvement, achievement, and success have no meaning." – Benjamin Franklin

Learning is perceived and generally acknowledged by those of us who have gone through primary and university tutoring. We were routinely encircled by people who energized and upheld our developments. Groundbreaking thoughts and change were anticipated from us; the sky was the limit!! However, shouldn't something be said about once we got into the work environment? For some, we subsided into the everyday daily practice, getting it done, uninformed of the cost that our agreeable, monotonous, continuous tasks appeared to have on our own and expert development.

Do you hear employees saying, "I don't get how this venture's development works" or "I'm awful at giving introductions. If it's not too much trouble, let another person do it." If this is the case, reconsideration of your group's growth mindset might be in order. They are working under a "fixed mentality." According to an examination concentrate via Carol Dweck of Stanford University, a fixed attitude happens when individuals accept fixed qualities that can't change. These individuals archive abilities instead of attempting to foster them. On the other hand, a development attitude accepts that knowledge can develop with time and experience. When individuals accept they can add to their learning, they understand exertion affects their prosperity.

You can attempt to battle a fixed attitude and energize a sound growth mindset by rehearsing the following:

Recognize fixed mindset patterns

To begin with, would you say you are ready to precisely recognize and uncover the negative quirks coming about because of a fixed mentality? Normal practices of these individuals incorporate the individuals who keep away from challenges, surrender effectively, consider there to be as achieving nothing, overlook and keep away from negative criticism, need heading in their objectives, and carry on when feeling undermined by other people who make progress. These are normal signs that employees are battling to see their part in supporting the new turn of events.

Energize feedback over praise

Commendation feels better. We like to feel approved in our qualities and are content to let it be the point at which we get acclaim over achieved work—employees to request input despite the result. There are consistent approaches to improve and create. Lead your group to request tips and innovative manners by which they can move toward new situations.

Pinpoint skills and limitations

Take time out from the ordinary daily schedule to pinpoint your workers' qualities and shortcomings will give an unmistakable beginning stage to an initiative in realizing where holes exist. Have workers independently take strength evaluations and meet with them to go over outcomes. Some may feel compromised and cautious while going over shortcomings, yet having a direct discussion on the finding will prompt better anticipation and recuperating.

Chapter 16:
Consistency Can Bring You Happiness

Happiness is an individual concept.

One man's riches is another man's rubbish.

As humans we are not happy if we do not have a routine, a reason to get up, and a purpose to live.

Without working towards something consistently, we become lost.

We begin to drift.

Drifting with no purpose eventually leads to emptiness.

When we are drifting in a job we hate,

We are trading our future away,

When we inconsistent in our relationships,

Problems are bound to arise.

Choose consistent focus instead.

Figure out exactly what you want and start to change it.

Employ consistent routines and habits that to move you towards your goals.

Consistency and persistence are key to success and happiness.

Without consistent disciplined effort towards what we want, we resign to a life of mediocrity.

Read a book for an hour consistently every single day.
You will become a national expert in 1 year.
In 5 years, a global expert.
That is the power of consistency.
Instead, people spend most of their free time scrolling through social media.

Consistency starts in the mind.
Control your thoughts to be positive despite the circumstances.
Nothing in the world can make us happy if we choose not to be.

Choose to be happy now and consistently working towards your goals.
We cannot be happy and successful if we dwell in the day to day setbacks.

We must consistently move like a bulldozer.
We have to keep going no matter what.
Nothing stays in the path of a bulldozer for too long.

In life, no matter where you are, you only ever have two choices.
Choose to stay where you are? Or choose to keep moving?

If where you are is making you happy, then by all means do more of it.
If not. What will? And why?
This should be clear before you take action.

Start with the end in your mind.
Let your body catch-up to it afterwards.
The end result is your what.
The action required is your how.
Concentrate on the what and the how and it will all be revealed soon enough.

Concentrate consistently on what you want for yourself and your family.
Distraction and lack of consistent action is a killer of happiness and success.
Your happiness is the life you want.
Take consistent action towards that life you've always dreamed of.
Commitment and endurance is part of that process.

On earth things need time to nurture and grow.
Everything in life depends on it.
The right conditions for maximum growth.

You can't just throw a seed on the concrete and expect it to grow with no soil and water,
Just as you can't simply wish for change and not create the right environment for success.

A seed requires not just consistent sunlight,
But the perfect combination of water and nutrients as well.
You might have given that seed sunlight,
just as you have your dream hope,

But without faith and consistent action towards the goal, nothing will happen.
The seed will still stay a seed forever.

Consistency in thought and action is everything towards happiness.
Nothing can grow without it.
Your success can be measured by your time spent working towards your goals.
If we consistently do nothing we become successful in nothing.
If we have to do something, should it not be something worth doing?

Start doing things that make you happy and fulfilled.
Consistency towards something that makes you happy is key towards lasting success.
Adapt when necessary but remain consistent with the end result in mind.
The path can be changed when necessary but the destination cannot.
Accepting anything less is admitting defeat.

Consistent concentration on the end result can and will be tested.
It however cannot be defeated, unless you quit.
If we remain steadfast in our belief that this is possible for us, it will be possible.
After a while things will seem probable. Eventually it becomes definite.

Continue to believe you can do it despite the circumstances.
Continue despite everyone around you saying you can't do it.

In spite of social status,

in spite of illness or disability,

in spite of age, race or nationality,

know you can do nearly anything if you consistently put all of your mind and body towards the task.

Take the pressure off.

There is no set guideline.

It is what you make of it.

There is no set destination or requirements.

Those are set my you.

The only competition is yourself from yesterday.

If you can consistently outperform that person, your success is guaranteed.

Consistent concentration and action towards your dream is key you your success and happiness.

Chapter 17:
<u>10 Habits of Muhammad Ali</u>

It has been five years since the Olympic gold-medallist, three-time heavyweight champion, and American hero Muhammad Ali passed away. Ali was a boxer, social activist, and philanthropist who is universally recognized as one of the greatest boxing champions of the twentieth century, with a record of 56 wins.

He is also renowned for his courageous, fierce opposition against the Vietnam War. Ali had a colorful life, fought for personal rights in the truest sense of the concept, and left behind a boxing legacy that will be remembered for centuries to come. His life was one of the most inspiring in modern history.

Here are the ten habits of Muhammad Ali.

1. Adopt a Growth Attitude

According to Dr. Dweck, Muhammad Ali's outstanding boxing career had considerably more to do with his growth-oriented psyche than the commonly accepted-yet incorrect-physical talent. Regardless of how lackluster his physical attributes were; his mind-game was on the fire. Instead of lamenting on how you're not enough, focus on embracing different paths to achieving greatness.

2. Affirm Your Beliefs Strongly

Ali's refusal to serve in Vietnam was premised on his respect for what he believed in. "I don't have a beef with the Viet Cong," he remarked. "Why should they expect me to put on a uniform... and drop bombs and bullets on brown people... while so-called Negroes in Louisville are treated like dogs and denied basic human rights?" This sentiment elevated Ali's status from prized heavyweight boxer to renowned civil rights figure. What about you? It's as simple as that: stay true to yourself and your ideas, no matter what they are.

3. Confidence Is Everything

Ali's remarkable "trash" talks before the fights were everything, and his antics enraged both fighters and fans. Sure, the sheer amount of confidence he exuded bordered on arrogance. But, based on his record, it's reasonable to assume that confidence can get you a long way. Give it a try: stand tall with your head held high.

4. It's Never Too Serious

In his memoir, Ali said that his most desired legacy was his sense of humor, which is evident in his cocky digs at other boxers and his poetic self-promotion. Even after Parkinson's disease, he remained as sharp as ever up to his death. This demonstrates the power of humor in defying human limits and spit in the face of adversity while making yourself youthful at heart.

5. Give Back

When you are given a voice, it is your responsibility to use it for others' benefit. Aside from being an unmistakable advocate for civil rights, Ali demonstrated his devotion to equality and positivism by taking on a plethora of humanitarian tasks - his negotiation for the release of numerous American prisoners in Iraq in 2001 is just one example.

6. Be Enthusiastic About Something

Ali was passionate about more than simply boxing. He was a devout Muslim who found great personal joy in his beliefs. Ali was a brilliant boxer, but he was also a fantastic person. Be enthusiastic about your own beliefs.

7. Say As You Mean It

When you look up at Muhammad's videos, you'll notice his proud, booming, and roaring voice while being interviewed, giving speeches, or even "trash" talking his opponents. This doesn't mean you go yelling at everyone at work, but a little timidity won't hurt. Try it: it's not entirely drilled sergeant, but it's also not precisely librarian.

8. Find and Pursue Your Purpose

Just like Ali, drag yourself to the gym before or after work, be productive at work (as much as possible), and try to make the most of your day. Every morning, get up with a sense of purpose.

9. Take Life By Its Horns

Ali's rise started as vengeance towards his stolen bike. Then came a Golden Gloves champion, an amateur champion, an Olympic gold medalist to having a long career as a three-time world heavyweight champion. What does this tell you? That you should always be hungry for more.

10. Have a Higher Goal

Muhammad once said, "you have one life; it will soon be over; what you do for God is all that will last," In order to have a meaningful and satisfying life, you must fulfil a higher purpose in your life.

Conclusion

The next time you find yourself at the crossroads between your comfort zone and unfamiliar terrain, remember these habits and imagine Muhammad Ali's heavy glove on your shoulder, softly but firmly pressing you to walk over the line.

Chapter 18:
Happy People Don't Make Excuses

"If you are interested, you'll do what's convenient. If you are committed, you'll do whatever it takes" — John Assaraff.

Read it again. Take it in. This is one of the most effective ideas I recognize in the making and proudly owning your fitness and happiness. Happy humans are dedicated to being satisfied and successful, and much less satisfied humans are normally simplest inquisitive about being satisfied.

The distinction is huge.

What it means is this. When we are truly committed to an outcome — whatever it may be: getting in shape, buying an investment property, qualifying as a vet, owning your own business — we will do whatever it takes to make it happen. There will be obstacles. With any milestone that's big or consequential, a few (or many) obstacles along the way are an inevitable part of that journey. A happy and successful person knows that and moves over or around that obstacle in whatever way they can to keep their eye focused on the outcome they want. They will try and try and try in however many ways they need to to make it happen. They are not just interested in their success, and they are incontrovertibly committed to it. They don't get thrown off at the first sign of struggle.

They are more committed to their goal than they are interested in another 45 minutes in bed or the social acceptance of joining in with a slice of cake.

When we are interested rather than committed, the main thing you will hear coming out of our mouths is excuses. "Oh, I was going to save that money, but something unexpected came up"; "I am getting back on that eating plan as soon as, but it's just been really busy at the moment" that sort of thing.
Excuses. Excuses.

This is the place where my other statement comes in, "Everything before the 'but' is BS." Smart, correct? It summarizes everything for me — everything before the "yet" is what we are keen on, instead of focusing on. On the off chance that we were submitted, there would be no "however." It would be an "and" all things being equal. For instance: "I needed to set aside that cash, something startling came up thus I needed to work three additional movements/offer some stuff to get it going" or "I'm back on that eating plan, it's been truly occupied right now thus I have needed to deny many things to get it going; however, I've done it."

Chapter 19:
Becoming High Achievers

By becoming high achievers we become high off life, what better feeling is there than aiming for something you thought was unrealistic and then actually hitting that goal.

What better feeling is there than declaring we will do something against the perceived odds and then actually doing it.

To be a high achiever you must be a believer,

You must believe in yourself and believe that dream is possible for you.

It doesn't matter what anyone else thinks , as long as you believe,

To be a high achiever we must hunger to achieve.

To be an action taker.

Moving forward no matter what.

High achievers do not quit.

Keeping that vision in their minds eye until it becomes reality, no matter what.

Your biggest dream is protected by fear , loss and pain.

We must conquer all 3 of these impostors to walk through the door.

Not many do , most are still fighting fear and if they lose the battle, they quit.

Loss and pain are part of life.

Losses are hard on all of us.

Whether we lose possessions, whether we lose friends, whether we lose our jobs, or whether we lose family members.

Losing doesn't mean you have lost.

Losses are may be a tough pill to swallow, but they are essential because we cannot truly succeed until we fail.

We can't have the perfect relationship if we stay in a toxic one, and we can't have the life we desire until we make room by letting go of the old.

The 3 imposters that cause us so much terror are actually the first signs of our success.

So walk through fear in courage , look at loss as an eventual gain, and know that the pain is part of the game and without it you would be weak.

Becoming a high achiever requires a single minded focus on your goal, full commitment and an unnatural amount of persistence and work.

We must define what high achievement means to us individually, set the bar high and accept nothing less.

The achievement should not be money as money is not our currency but a tool.

The real currency is time and your result is the time you get to experience the world's places and products , so the result should always be that.

The holiday home , the fast car and the lifestyle of being healthy and wealthy, those are merely motivations to work towards. Like Carrots on a stick.

High achievement is individual to all of us, it means different things to each of us,

But if we are going to go for it we might as well go all out for the life we want, should we not?

I don't think we beat the odds of 1 in 400 trillion to be born, just to settle for mediocrity, did we?

Being a high achiever is in your DNA, if you can beat the odds, you can beat anything.

It is all about self-belief and confidence, we must have the confidence to take the action required and often the risk.

Risk is difficult for people and it's a difficult tight rope to walk. The line between risk and recklessness is razor thin.

Taking risks feels unnatural, not surprisingly as we all grew up in a health and safety bubble with all advice pointing towards safe and secure ways. But the reward is often in the risk and sometimes a leap of blind faith is required. This is what stops most of us - the fear of the unknown.

The truth is the path to success is foggy and we can only ever see one step ahead, we have to imagine the result and know it's somewhere down this foggy path and keep moving forward with our new life in mind.

Know that we can make it but be aware that along the path we will be met by fear, loss and pain and the bigger our goal the bigger these monsters will be.

The top achievers financially are fanatical about their work and often work 100+ hours per week.

Some often work day and night until a project is successful.

Being a high achiever requires giving more than what is expected, standing out for the high standard of your work because being known as number 1 in your field will pay you abundantly.

Being an innovator, thinking outside the box for better practices, creating superior products to your competition because quality is more rewarding than quantity.

Maximizing the quality of your products and services to give assurance to your customers that your company is the number 1 choice.

What can we do differently to bring a better result to the table and a better experience for our customers?

We must think about questions like that because change is inevitable and without thinking like that we get left behind, but if we keep asking that, we can successfully ride the wave of change straight to the beach of our desired results.

The route to your success is by making people happy because none of us can do anything alone, we must earn the money and to earn it we must make either our employers or employees and customers happy.

To engage in self-promotion and positive interaction with those around us, we must be polite and positive with everyone, even with our competition.

Because really the only competition is ourselves and that is all we should focus on.

Self-mastery, how can I do better than yesterday?

What can I do different today that will improve my circumstances for tomorrow.

Little changes add up to a big one.

The belief and persistence towards your desired results should be 100%, I will carry on until… is the right attitude.

We must declare to ourselves that we will do this , we don't yet know how but we know that we will.

Because high achievers like yourselves know that to make it you must endure and persist untill you win.

High achievers have an unnatural grit and thick skin , often doing what others won't, putting in the extra hours when others don't.

After you endure loss and conquer pain , the sky is the limit, and high achievers never settle until they are finished.

Chapter 20:
8 Ways On How To Start Taking Actions

Have you ever got caught up in situations when you can't bring yourself moving from deciding to doing? As a famous person once said, "Your beliefs become your thoughts; your thoughts become your words; your words become your actions; your actions become your habits; your habits become your values; your values become your destiny."

The first step towards success is by taking action. If you keep on thinking that you have to lose weight, start a business, learn a new language, or get another degree, you will end up nowhere without executing these thoughts into actions.

Here are 8 Ways To Start Moving The Needle In Your Life:

1. Decide that you want to get out of your comfort zone

The fear that we have that doesn't allow us to take action is that we might have to sacrifice our comfort zone in the process. And trust me, a lot of people aren't willing to do that. But if you don't step out of your comfort zone, how will you determine your true potential? You don't need the motivation to start taking action, and you just have to gather your willpower, stop with the excuses and procrastination, and get moving!

2. **Don't indulge in the habit of Hesitatation**

Have you had a great idea but then decide 10 minutes later that it was stupid. Ever wondered why that was? The answer is quite simple and straightforward; hesitation. We dwell on hesitation for too long. This makes it very difficult for us to get started on something. Thinking will only lead us to more and more thinking, which will lead us to a loop of continual thoughts, and our actions will get dominated by them. And then the regret that follows us is usually, "Why didn't we start earlier?" David Joseph Schwartz once said, "To fight fear, act. To increase fear – wait, put off, postpone."

3. **Stop waiting for the perfect time:**

There's a Chinese proverb that says, "The best time to plant a tree was 20 years ago. The second-best time is now." It means that there is no such thing as perfect timing. The minute we start to take action, the time becomes perfect. If we wait till everything gets in order or becomes exemplary, then we will be waiting forever. The ideal time in your eyes was last year, but the second-best time is right here and right now. It's never too late to start with your goals, dreams, and passions. All we have in our hands is the present time and what counts is how efficiently we spend this time. We must take action now and make adjustments along the way if we feel like it.

4. **Don't pause and wait:**

Have you ever found yourself thinking that, hey, it's a good day to wander around the city, but found yourself sitting and wasting time watching TV? Or you thought of doing your assignment but got caught up in a more hopeless task? Or you thought of presenting a new idea to your boss but got shied away? All of these thoughts, no matter how positive they were, stand nowhere unless you implement them. So stop being a talker and start being a doer. A doer is someone who immediately moves forward with his ideas. When we pause and look around, we will find ourselves making excuses and allow doubts to creep through into our minds. "The most difficult thing is the decision to act; the rest is merely tenacity." - Amelia Earhart.

5. **Stop Over-thinking:**

There's always an endless loop of overthinking that we can't get over with no matter how hard we try. From imagining the worst-case scenarios of even the best situations to getting anxious and depressed whenever any minor inconvenience happens, our mind tricks us into thinking that we can never get the best of both worlds (HM fans, I gotcha!) When we overthink stuff, we tend to get paralysis of analysis. We start to analyze every situation and obsess over how things aren't perfect, or the conditions aren't going our way. We question the amount of time that we have to commit and make endless excuses and reasons not to move forward with whatever we want to do.

6. Take continuous action:

The first step is the hardest step that we have to take. But once you get started, make sure that you fully commit yourself to your goal. Take continuous actions and keep up with your momentum by doing something related to your plan every day. Even if you are scheduling only 15-20 minutes of your life completing a small task, it will eventually add up into the more remarkable things. Moreover, it will help you build confidence by seeing your achievements. "It does not matter how slowly you go as long as you do not stop." - Confucius.

7. Overcome your fears:

We often succumb to our fears before even taking a step. The fear of failure, of not being good enough, of not doing enough, is the most common among them. Our mind tricks us into thinking that we might end up failing sooner or later. This prevents us from taking the first step and implementing our thoughts into actions. For example, suppose you're a professional speaker at a public speaking event. You have gained loads of experience, and you have no problem speaking to the lobby. But you do feel yourself getting nervous when you have to wait around for your turn. However, once you get started, all that fear and anxiety disappear. If you face similar situations in life, start being a doer, take action towards it and see how it will boost your confidence.

8. Eliminate any distractions:

We live in a world where distractions and procrastination have become more important than productivity. Have you ever found yourself thinking that you will take the online lecture for the subject you have been struggling with but ended up checking your social media accounts or watching irrelevant videos on YouTube? Procrastination is the primary reason we never end up doing what we should keep in our priorities. Instead, we should focus on our tasks, eliminate all the distractions and start with a slow but steady pace towards our goal. A single average idea put into action is far more valuable than those 20 genius ideas saved for another day or another time.

Conclusion:

Achieving your goals and dreams isn't an overnight task but takes years and decades to give you the final fruits. It's a road that will have setbacks, obstacles, lessons, and challenges. But what matters is that we shouldn't give up. We should face all the struggles and not surrender ourselves to our fears and demotivation. Converting your thoughts into actions and then enjoying the journey will equip you to thrive and see your goals become a reality in no time. So take into account what steps you took today. No matter how small they may be, appreciate and celebrate them.

Chapter 21:
Happy People Create Time to Do What They Love Every Day

Most of our days are filled with things that we need to do and the things we do to destress ourselves. But, in between all this, we never get time for things. We wanted to do things that bring us pure joy. So then the question is, When will we find time to do what we love? Then, when things calm down a bit and when the people who visit us leave or finish all the trips we have planned and wrap up our busy projects, and the kids will be grown, we will retire? Then, probably after we are dead, we will have more time.

You do not have to wait for things to get less busy or calmer. There will always be something coming up; trips, chores, visitors, errands, holidays, projects, death and illness. There is never going to be more time. Whatever you have been stuck in the past few years, it will always be like that. So now the challenge is not waiting for things to change it is to make time for things you love no matter how busy your life is. Sit down and think about what you want to do, something that you have been putting off. What is something that makes you feel fulfilled and happy? Everyone has those few things that make them fall in love with life think of what is that for you. If you haven't figured it out yet, we will give you some examples, and maybe you can try some of these things and see how that makes you feel.

- Communing with nature

- Going for a beautiful walk

- Creating or growing a business or an organization

- Hiking, running, biking, rowing, climbing

- Meditating, journaling, doing yoga, reflecting

- Communing with loved ones

- Crafting, hogging, blogging, logging, vlogging
- Reading aloud to kids
- Reading aloud to kids

Did you remember something you enjoyed doing, but as the responsibilities kept increasing, you sidelined it. Well, this is your sign to start doing what you loved to take time out for that activity every day, even if it is for 30 minutes only. Carve that time out for yourself, do it now. Once you start doing this, you will realize that you will have more energy because your brain will release serotonin, and your energy level will increase. Secondly, your confidence will improve because you will be making something love every day, and that will constantly help you gain confidence because you will be putting yourself in a happy, self-loving state. You will notice that you have started enjoying life more when you do something you love once a day. It makes the rest of your day brighter and happier. You will also want to constantly continue learning and growing because your brain will strive to do more and more of the thing you like to do, and that will eventually lead to an increased desire of learning and growing. Lastly, your motivation will soar because you will have something to look forward to that brings you pure joy.

Chapter 22: Happy People Are Proactive About Relationships

Researchers have found that as human beings we are only capable of maintaining up to 150 meaningful relationships, including five primary, close relationships.

This holds true even with the illusion of thousands of "friends" on social media platforms such as Facebook, Instagram, and Twitter. If you think carefully about your real interactions with people, you'll find the five close/150 extended relationships rule holds true.

Perhaps not coincidentally, Tony Robbins, the personal development expert, and others argue that your attitudes, behavior, and success in life are the sum total of your five closest relationships. So, toxic relationships, toxic life.

With this in mind, it's essential to continue to develop relationships that are positive and beneficial. **But in today's distracted world, these relationships won't just happen.**

We need to be proactive about developing our relationships.

My current favorite book on personal development is Tim Ferriss's excellent, though long, 700+ page book, *Tools of Titans: The Tactics, Routines, and Habits of Billionaires, Icons, and World-Class Performers.*

At one point, Ferriss quotes retired women's volleyball great Gabby Reece:

I always say that I'll go first.... That means if I'm checking out at the store, I'll say "hello" first. If I'm coming across somebody and make eye contact, I'll smile first. [I wish] people would experiment with that in their life a little bit: be first, because – not all times, but most times – it comes in your favor... The response is pretty amazing.... I was at the park the other day with the kids.

Oh, my God. Hurricane Harbor [water park]. It's like hell. There were these two women a little bit older than me. We couldn't be more different, right? And I walked by them, and I just looked at them and smiled. The smile came to their face so instantly. They're ready, but you have to go first because now we're being trained in this world [to opt out] – nobody's going first anymore.

Be proactive: start the conversation

I agree. I was excited to read this principle because I adopted this by default years ago, and it's given me the opportunity to hear the most amazing stories and develop the greatest relationships you can imagine.

On airplanes, in the grocery store, at lunch, I've started conversations that led to trading heartfelt stories, becoming friends, or doing business together. A relationship has to start someplace, and that can be any place in any moment.

Be proactive: lose your fear of being rejected

I also love this idea because it will help overcome one of the main issues I hear from my training and coaching clients – the fear of making an initial connection with someone they don't know.

This fear runs deep for many people and may be hardwired in humans. We are always observing strangers to determine if we can trust them – whether they have positive or dangerous intent.

In addition, **we fear rejection. Our usual negative self-talk says something like,** *If I start the conversation, if I make eye contact, if I smile, what if it's not returned?*

What if I'm rejected, embarrassed, or ignored by no response? I'll feel like an idiot, a needy loser.

Chapter 23:
If You Commit to Nothing, You'll Be Distracted By Everything

I don't think anyone in their right mind would like to face a challenge where they have a chance to face failure or even a possibility of it.

We all need a new lesson to learn. A lesson of commitment and conviction. A lesson of integrity, grit, and sheer will. One might ask, why should I adopt the features of a soldier rather than a normal social being. Why do I need to go to extremes?

The answer to these questions is simple yet heavy, with a load most people avoid their whole life.

We all have somewhat similar goals. We all want to be in a better place in better shape. We all want wealth. We all want healthy stable relationships. We all want respect and a million other things.

Ask yourself this; Have you ever actually tried hard enough for any of this to happen. Have you ever tried to dig deep till you found your last breath? But it felt good because you had a good enough reason and passion to pursue?

The goals of life are a compulsion to have. We all must have something to strive for. Something worth fighting for. Something we can look back and be happy about.

But having a goal and committing to it are two different things.

One can have a goal and still not be motivated enough to do anything in their power to achieve that thing. No matter how the road takes turns.

We need to have the inspiration to drive us through the rough patches of life. To make us keep pushing even if we get squeezed within the incidents happening around us.

Don't take this the wrong way but you have to accept the fact that whatever you are feeling has nothing to do with what you want to achieve. Because what you want to achieve is something that your life depends on. The goals you set aren't some wishes or a feeling that your gut gives you. These goals are the requirements of life with which you can finally say lived a happy successful life. And this statement is the ultimate purpose of your life.

You were given this life because you had the energy to go for things that weren't easy, but you had the potential to achieve these. All you needed was a little commitment and Zero distractions.

The commitment you need isn't a feeling that goes and on and off like a switch. Rather a distinct key for the lock of your life.

So if you still think you will have days where you can try one more time, Let me be clear; You better start thinking about the future of your next generation. Because I don't think they'd have one.

You need to be committed enough to do anything that takes you closer and closer to your goals and nothing that wastes a second out of your life.

Because either you go all in or you walk the line and hedge your bets. The bet here being your life.

Chapter 24:
How to Eat With Mood in Mind

At the point when you're feeling down, it tends to be enticing to go to food to lift your spirits. Notwithstanding, the sweet, fatty treats that numerous individuals resort to have unfortunate results of their own. Along these lines, you may puzzle over whether any good food sources can work on your temperament.

As of late, research on the connection between sustenance and psychological wellness has been arising. However, note that state of mind can be impacted by numerous variables, like pressure, climate, helpless rest, hereditary qualities, mood disorders, and nutritional deficiencies. In any case, certain food varieties have been displayed to further develop general mental wellbeing and specific kinds of temperament issues.

1. Fatty Fish
Omega-3 unsaturated fats are a gathering of fundamental fats you should get through your eating routine because your body can't produce them all alone. Fatty fish like salmon and tuna fish are wealthy in two sorts of omega-3s — docosahexaenoic corrosive (DHA) and eicosapentaenoic corrosive (EPA) — that are connected to bring down degrees of despair. Omega-3s add to lower your depression and seem to assume key parts in mental health and cell flagging.

2. Dark Chocolate

Chocolate is wealthy in numerous mood-boosting compounds. Its sugar may further develop mood since it's a fast wellspring of fuel for your brain. Besides, it's anything but a course of feel-great mixtures, like caffeine, theobromine, and N-acylethanolamine — a substance synthetically like cannabinoids that have been connected to improved mood.

3. Fermented Food Varieties

Fermented food sources, which incorporate kimchi, yogurt, kefir, fermented tea, and sauerkraut, may further develop gut wellbeing and state of mind. The fermentation interaction permits live microbes to flourish in food varieties ready to change over sugars into liquor and acids. During this interaction, probiotics are made. These live microorganisms support the development of solid microscopic organisms in your gut and may expand serotonin levels.

4. Bananas

Bananas may assist with flipping around a frown.

They're high in nutrient B6, which orchestrates feel-great synapses like dopamine and serotonin.

Moreover, one enormous banana (136 grams) gives 16 grams of sugar and 3.5 grams of fiber.

When matched with fiber, sugar is delivered gradually into your circulation system, considering stable glucose levels and better disposition control. Glucose levels that are too low may prompt irritability and emotional episodes.

5. Oats

Oats are an entire grain that can keep you feeling great the entire morning. You can appreciate them in numerous structures, like, for the time being, oats, oatmeal, muesli, and granola. They're a phenomenal wellspring of fiber, giving 8 grams in a solitary crude cup (81 grams). Fiber eases back your processing of carbs, considering a slow arrival of sugar into the circulation system to keep your energy levels stable.

Chapter 25:
How To Crush Your Goals This Quarter

Some people find it very hard to achieve their goals, but luckily, there is a method waiting to be used. The quarter method divides the year into four parts of 90-days; for each part, you set some goals to crush. The rest of the year has gone, and so have the three quarters; now it is time to prepare for the fourth quarter. 1st October is one of the most critical days in the life of a person who sets his goals according to the quarter. It is the benchmark representing the close of the third quarter and the beginning of the fourth quarter. It is the day when you set new goals for the upcoming three months; if somehow your third-quarter dreams were not crushed, then you can stage a comeback so you wouldn't be left behind forever. But how to achieve your fourth-quarter goals?

1st October may bring the start of a quarter, but it also ends another quarter; it is the day when you focus on your results. Have you achieved the goals you set for the third quarter? If not, then prepare yourself to hear the hard truth. Your results reflect your self-esteem; if you believe in yourself, then you would achieve your goals. If you are not satisfied with your results, think, is this what you had in mind? If no, then having small visions can never lead to a more significant impact. Limiting beliefs will never give you more than minor and unimpressive results. Your results tell you about your passion for your work; if you are not passionate about your work, you would have poor outcomes. We all have heard the famous saying, " work in silence and let your success make the noise," but what does this mean? It means that your results will tell everyone about your hard work. If your results are not satisfactory, you know that the problem is your behavior towards your work.

When setting goals for the future, one needs to accept the facts; what went wrong that put you off the track? The year is 75% complete, and if you still haven't crushed your goals, you need to accept that it is your fault. If you blame these failures on your upbringing, your education, or any other factor than yourself, then you are simply fooling yourself because it is all dependent on you. When you don't achieve what you wanted to in nine months, you must have figured the problem; it can be any bad habit you are not willing to give up or the strategies you are implying. If you pretend your habits, attitude, and approach are just fine, you are just fooling yourself, not anyone else. This benchmark is the best time to change the old bad habits and try forming some new strategies.

To finish the year with solid results, you need to get serious; the days of dissatisfied results are gone, now it is time to shine some light on your soul and determine what you are doing wrong, what habits are working in your favor, and which ones are not. Then you can decide which habits to give up on, which habits to improve, and which ones to keep. Once you have sorted this out, prioritize your goals and set some challenging destinations to avoid getting bored or feeling uninterested. When setting deadlines, try to set enforceable deadlines.

Confusion can lead to poor results, so sit back and think about the goals that I should not pursue. This is called understanding goal competition; the goals you set are competing for your time. Actual peak performance comes from understanding which goals to pursue and which not to seek. And when you complete a plan, don't just rush into the process of crushing the next goal; allow yourself to celebrate your win and feel the happiness of the goal finally getting destroyed by you.

Chapter 26:
Happy People Choose to Exercise

There is a feeling you get when you just finish your workout, and you feel amazing, much better than you were feeling before. Even when you are not feeling motivated to go to the gym, just thinking about this feeling makes you get up, leave your bed and get going to the gym. This feeling can also be called an endorphin rush. Exercise indeed makes you happier in multiple ways.

Firstly, movement helps you bond with others that are in the brain chemistry of it all. Your heart rate is going up, you are using your body, engaging your muscles, your brain chemistry will change, and it will make it easier for you to connect and bond with other people. It also changes how your trust people. Research also showed that social pressures like a hug, laughing, or high-five are also enhanced. You will also find your new fitness fam, the people you will be working out with, and because you will have a shared interest that is having a healthy lifestyle will help you have a stronger bond with them. And as experts say that having strong relationships and connections in life will help you in overall happiness.

We have already discussed those exercise increases endorphins but what you do not know is that it increases a lot more brain chemicals that make you feel happy and good about yourself. Some of the brain chemicals that increase are; dopamine, endorphins, endocannabinoid and adrenaline. All of these chemicals are associated with feeling confident, capable, and happy. The amount of stress, physical pain, and anxiety also decrease significantly. A chemical that your body creates when your muscles contract is called "myokine", it is also shown to boost happiness and relieve stress.

Secondly, exercise can help boost your confidence, and of course, when it comes to feeling empowered and happy, confidence is the key. "At the point when you move with others, it's anything but a solid feeling of 'greater than self' probability that causes individuals to feel more idealistic and enabled, "Also, it permits individuals to feel more engaged turning around the difficulties in their own lives. What's more, that is a fascinating side advantage of moving with others because there's an encapsulated feeling of 'we're in the same boat' that converts into self-assurance and the capacity to take on difficulties in your day; to day existence."

Thirdly, exercising outdoors affects your brain, similar to meditation. In case you're similar to the innumerable other people who have found out about the advantages of contemplation yet can't make the time, uplifting news. You may not need to contemplate to get a portion of the advantages. Researchers found that exercising outside can similarly affect the cerebrum and disposition as reflection. Exercising outside immediately affects a state of mind that is amazingly incredible for wretchedness and nervousness. Since it's anything but a state in your mind that is the same as contemplation, the condition of open mindfulness,"

Chapter 27:
10 Habits of Cristiano Ronaldo

Cristiano Ronaldo dos Santos Aveiro, famously known as Cristiano Ronaldo, was born on 5th February 1985 in Funchal, Madeira, Portugal. He is the last born in a family of four children. His father, José Dinis Aveiro, named the football legend after his favorite actor – Ronald Reagan.

Here are ten habits of Cristiano Ronaldo:

1. <u>He pursues his dreams.</u>

Nothing stands in the way of Ronaldo and his dreams. In an interview with British reporters, his godfather – Fernao Sousa – recalls how young Ronaldo loved soccer. He could escape out of his bedroom window with a ball when he ought to be doing his homework. He could even skip meals to go play soccer.

Cristiano Ronaldo has played for great clubs like Manchester United, Real Madrid, Juventus and his national team – Portugal.

2. <u>He knows how to package himself.</u>

Cristiano Ronaldo is one of the highly paid professional soccer players globally. Manchester United paid £12.24 million for young Ronaldo and he joined the club on 12th August 2003. It was a lot of money for a teenager but his expertise in soccer was unmatched.

On 11th June 2009, he left Manchester United for Real Madrid after the latter paid $131 million! His transfer from the London club was imminent but nobody expected such a high price could be paid for his services.

3. <u>He is hardworking.</u>

Ronaldo trains hard to play the best football game ever. His performance with Portugal against Manchester United amazed everybody and the club signed the young player after some of their players asked their manager to do so.

He told reporters that he was aware of the pressure to perform he would have at Real Madrid but he was up to the task. He confessed that he was ready for new challenges for him to become the best footballer.

4. <u>He knows how to handle victory.</u>

Cristiano Ronaldo has not let victory cloud his judgement. He has maintained his rationality despite being the world's most celebrated soccer player. He knows the responsibility on his shoulders of being a role model to many people globally.

He has bagged many awards in his football career including best Fifa Men's player (twice), ballon d'or (five times), UEFA best player in Europe (thrice), European champion, Champions league winner (five times) and many more. Cristiano Ronaldo has guarded himself from pride despite global recognition and all the accolades he has won.

5. <u>He knows how to keep things private.</u>

Ronaldo is a global football icon and his life is constantly under constant watch. It is almost impossible for him to live a private life. He is aware of this and has tried a lot to keep his personal life under wraps.

He has kept the status of his relationship to Georgina Rodriguez private with Italian media speculating that they had wed in Morocco. The couple has not come out to clear the air. The only information in the public is that they have a daughter together.

6. <u>He loves parenting.</u>

The football superstar loves parenting. He is not an absentee father. His relationship with his children is very good. He often trains his son – Cristiano junior – how to play soccer like him. A video of Ronaldo senior training with Ronaldo junior garnered 4 million views in 30 minutes on Instagram.

It is evident that the five times ballon d'or winner is doing a good job as a parent and coach because his son has scored 58 goals in only 28 games for the under-9s in Juventus.

7. <u>He is responsible.</u>

Cristiano Ronaldo is a responsible person. When he was still in Juventus, Massimiliano Allegri, tasked Ronaldo with the responsibility of inspiring the younger players in the team.

He confessed that Ronaldo is a great player and smart guy. He has never been the team captain at Juventus nor at Manchester United but he is a responsible team player and has been coordinating the team within and without the pitch.

8. **He values family.**

Ronaldo has demonstrated the importance of family. He had a close relationship with his father until the former succumbed to kidney related problems. He wanted his father to go to rehab to cure his alcoholism addiction but he declined his son's offer.

The football star has also taken care of his family by buying them a property worth £ 7 million in Portugal. He prioritizes the well-being of his family over anything in his life.

9. **He is generous.**

Cristiano is a generous man. He once sold a golden boot award in an auction that raised more than a million Euros. The proceeds were channeled towards building schools in Gaza. He similarly auctioned his award for best player of the year in 2017 and the funds were donated to the Make-A-Wish foundation.

He recently took a pay cut from March to June 2021 that cost him 3.8 million euros. He has also donated almost one million euros to hospitals in Portugal aid in the fight against the coronavirus pandemic.

10. **He is patriotic.**

Ronaldo is a patriotic citizen to his motherland, Portugal. He has lead the national soccer team to the world cup several times and also in European tournaments as the team captain. It is conspicuous that he has never been the team captain for any of the football clubs he has played for.

He accepted to pay a £ 16.6 million fine over tax evasion charges. He acted how a patriotic citizen would do instead of battling it in court to maneuver the charges against him.

In conclusion, these are the ten habits of the world's soccer G.O.A.T (greatest of all time).

Chapter 28:
10 Habits of Jack Ma

It takes a special person to amass a total net worth of more than $20 billion through hard work and keeping a sense of perspective. Alibaba, one of world's largest e-commerce online platforms, Ceo and founder, Jack Ma is one of the world's wealthiest people, but his success hasn't clouded his strategic direction. Jack Ma's success habits will truly inspire you whether you are an aspiring billionaire or you're a small-business entrepreneur.

To grow his e-commerce business, Jack overcame all difficulties. He had a rough upbringing in communist China. He also failed the college admissions exams twice and was turned down by more than a dozen businesses. He had previously created two failed Internet businesses. However, the third time, Alibaba took off swiftly.

Here are 10 things you can grasps from Jack Ma success journey:

1. Giving Up is Failing

Jack Ma is one person who understands the meaning of failure, as it started in his early days. He founded two companies which terribly failed before the success of Alibaba. For Ma, giving up is failure.

Give your grind your best shot even when the struggle is real. Failing shouldn't make you give up, instead make sure you see the goal through to the end. Hardship is your learning lesson, and understanding its lessons is the key to fortune.

2. Let Your Initiative Impact on Society Positively

Ma created his vision focusing on its impactful influence on consumers. He also notes that consumer's happiness should be the end goal rather than the profits.

Let your entrepreneurial path be the reason why people's lives are improving. This results will be in long-term-positive business relationships.

3. What's Matters Is Where You Finish

Your humble beginnings shouldn't prevent you from taking chances. Your spirit, toughness, grit, and fortitude will tell whether or not you'll succeed.

What matters is whether you are putting much effort as needed and this will tell how determined you are to succeed. Dig in your heels, like Jack Ma, and give every opportunity your all.

4. Act Swiftly

According to Jack Ma, you must be extremely quick in seizing opportunities. To win in the end, you must first be off the starting line. You must also be quick to recover from and learn from mistakes. Grab an opportunity that is in your line of sight as soon as you see it and work with it before anyone else does. This will elevate you above your competitors, who are merely competent.

5. Persistence

Ma believes that leaders must be tenacious and with a clear vision. Understanding what you want and having the drive to pursue it will not only put you on the path to success, but will also inspire those around you to work hard to achieve their goals. Ma's business concept is around taking pleasure in one's job and refusing to accept no for an answer.

6. Foresightedness

A good leader, according to Jack Ma, should have foresight. As a leader, it's good that you're always one step ahead of the competition by anticipating how decisions will be implemented before others. Invest your time in developing creative strategies while intensifying a trait where you always follow a knowledge-based intuition.

7. Take a risk

Ma founded Alibaba Group, a very successful conglomerate of internet enterprises, in the face of skepticism from potential investors. The perfect time to take risks, is when you are pursuing your chosen goal path-when criticism is at its core.

8. Be Prepared to Fail

Jack Ma is no stranger to failure. He applied to college three times before being accepted. He created two unsuccessful companies before success of Alibaba. Even KFC didn't think he was a good fit.

When you give up on your first try, you are turning your life around. As probably you'll move on to something else while ending your dreams.

9. Take Chances When You're Still Young

Ma believes that if you are not wealthy by the age of 35, you have squandered your youth. Take use of your youth's vitality and imagination by succumbing to your goal and pursuing it.

Accept and learn from every opportunity that comes your way while you're still young. Grab every opportunity and make best of it by giving it your all. Your ability to pick up any job will help you develop tenancy.

10. Live life

Ma has a reputation for not taking things too seriously. Despite his hectic schedule, he always finds time to relax and enjoy life. If you work your whole life, you will undoubtedly come to regret it.

Conclusion

Jack Ma is one of most inspiring person in the world. His struggle way up and desire for wealth continues to inspire. Through his experience, Jack Ma demonstrates how as an entrepreneur, you can bring ambition to life.

Chapter 29: Happy People Celebrate Other People's Success

What a phony smile… Why do people want him? How has he accomplished anything? It's ME they need. I'm the one who should be successful, not him. What a joke." This was my inner dialogue when I heard about other people's success. Like a prima donna, I seethed with jealousy and couldn't stand to hear about people doing better than me.

But all the hating got me nowhere. So I thought about who I was really mad at…it wasn't the successful people I raged at. When I got more serious about succeeding, I channeled that useless envy into accepting myself.

I practiced self-acceptance with a journal, through affirmations, and by encouraging myself—especially when I failed. Then something weird happened. I started feeling happy for other people's success. Without a hint of irony, I congratulated people on their hard work, and I applauded their success with my best wishes. It felt good. I felt more successful doing it.

> "Embrace your uniqueness. Time is much too short to be living someone else's life." – Kobi Yamada

My writing career caught fire at the same time. I was published on sites that I'd only dreamt of, and whose authors I had cussed for doing things that the egotistical me still hadn't. Congratulating others started a positive feedback loop. The more I accepted myself, the more I celebrated other people's success and the more I celebrated their success, the more success I achieved. Now that I look back, I could've hacked my growth curve by celebrating others' success as a daily ritual.

1. It conditions you for your own success

Feeling good for someone else's success helps you generate the same feelings you need for your own accomplishments. So put yourself in the other's shoes. Revel in their accomplishments; think of all the hard work that went into it. Celebrate their success and know that soon you'll experience the same thing for yourself. Apply the good feelings to your visions for a brighter future.

2. You'll transcend yourself

Everyone knows that to actually succeed, you need to be part of something bigger. But most people are kept from that bigger something by wanting all the focus for themselves. it's an ego issue.

Through celebrating others, you'll practice the selflessness it takes to let go of your tiny shell and leap into the ocean of success that comes through serving others. Cheer your fellow entrepreneurs. Feel their success. Let go of your want for recognition and accept that you'll get it when you help enough other people.

Chapter 30:
Become A High Performer

We were put on this planet because we were meant to be all we could become. Human beings are the sum of their acts and achievements. But not everyone is capable of doing things to their full potential.

Every man's biggest burden is his or her unfulfilled potential.

So what you need to become a high-performing individual in this modern era of competition is to idolize the best of the best.

You will need to understand the real-life features of a successful individual and what you need to do to become one.

If you want to be more successful in your life you need to become obsessive. Start your day with a goal and try your best to achieve it before you head to bed. You don't necessarily need to be on the right path with the first step, but you will find the best route once you have the undefeated will to find that path.

If you want to be more developed in your life you need to sleep effectively. The most successful people have a mantra of high performing routine. They don't sleep more than five hours a day and work seven days a week. They only take one day a week to sleep more just to rejuvenate their brains and body.

If you want to know if you are a high-performing successful person, look into your body language. If you find ease and leisure in everyday tasks, You are surely not standing up to your potential. If you like to sit for a conversation, start to stand. If you like to walk, start running. Get out of your comfort zone and start thinking and acting differently.

The last thing before you start your search for the right path to excellence is to set a goal every day. Increase your creativity by finding new ways to shorten the time of you becoming the better you and finally getting what you deserve.

You will eventually start seeing your life get on the track of productive learning and execution.

Change your way of treating others, especially those who are below you. If you are not a jolly person when you are broke, you can never be a jolly person when you are rich.

Never underestimate someone who is below you. You never know to whom the inspiration might take you. You have to consider the fact that life is ever-changing. Nothing ever stays the same. People never stay where they are for long.

It is the alternating nature of life that makes you keep fighting and pushing harder for better days. That is why you work hard on your skills to become a hearty human with the arms of steel.

Most people live a quiet life of desperation where they have a lot to give and a lot to say but can never get out of their cocoons.

But you are not every other person. You are the most unique soul god has created to excel at something no one has ever thought or seen before.

Start loving yourself. Stop finding faults in yourself. You are the best version of yourself, you just haven't found the right picture to look into it yet.

You want to be a high performer in every aspect of your life, here is my final advice for you.

If you push your limits in even the smallest tasks of your life, if you stretch your mind and imagination, if you can push the rules to your benefit, you might be the happiest and the most successful man humankind has ever seen.

Keep working for your dreams till the day you die. Life opens its doors to the people who knock on it. The purpose of this life is to knock on every door of opportunity and grasp that opportunity before anyone else steps forward.

You won't fulfill your desires till you make the desired effort, and that comes with a strong will and character. So keep doing what you want to never have a regret.

Chapter 31:
<u>7 Ways Your Behaviors Are Holding You Back</u>

Habits and behaviors are what defines a human being and make you who you are. It is what shapes us and defines our lives while making us move towards our future. However, did you know that there are multiple things that hold you back?

These are the behavior that molds us, defines us, holds us back to be the better person and achieves everything that it takes to be perfect. Well, not that anyone is perfect; however, we all can aspire to be! Isn't it so? Let us explore and discuss the ways that your behaviors hold you back.

1. Not Accepting Your Faults

We have all been guilty of doing the same. Haven't we? I am so sure that each one of you has at least once committed this sin of shifting the blame to someone else and removing it off your shoulders. We are humans, after all; we are governed by our hearts, more than our minds. This is why we are more inclined to never accepting our faults instead of putting the blame on others.

Irrespective of the circumstance, it is necessary that you accept your fault, realize your weakness, and evaluate what needs to be done in order to never repeat the same. Going forward, you must find a way to turn your weakness into strength.

2. Having Self-Doubt

A lot of us are seen killing our dreams due to fear of being rejected. Haven't you already done the same a few times? Well, we all have! Self-doubt is one of the silent killers that can do you more harm than any good. If you constantly find yourself doubting your potential and stuck in a negative situation, you need to know that you are holding yourself back.

You can only look forward and attain a prosperous tomorrow when you stop doubting yourself. Self-doubt can be highly injurious, and this is one big reason why you need to stop holding yourself back and take a giant leap forward, or maybe a baby step! Shall we?

3. Procrastinating On Everything

No matter how many times we decide not to keep doing it, we keep doing it! Let's face it, and there are way too many distractions for us to procrastinate and sideline our current goals and duties. Say hello to social media! It distracts you way too many times than it should, especially when you are on the verge of serving your last-minute deadlines!

Hasn't it already got way too annoying? If it has, you must take a deep breath and train your mind. This is one of the behaviors that might hold you back. When you find yourself in such a situation, you must stop procrastinating; instead, do what you are supposed to do. Doing this will help you largely concentrate and uplift productivity.

4. Disrespecting Others

Do you often find yourself engaging in putting others down? If yes, then let me tell you that you are only inviting a lot of ill wrath for yourself. Imagine telling yourself that you are incapable, you are not good enough, and stuffs similar.

Similarly, if you do the same things to others, you are dragging everyone down. This is why you must stop being the harsh person that you are being and put your negativity aside. Disrespecting others or putting others down will only do more harm to you and your mental well-being. Why not focus more on what you can do to uplift others, encourage others and bring in more positivity around yourself!

5. Being In Your Cozy Corner

Not literally, but what we mean is you being in your own comfort zone! We all need our own comfort zones to feel safe and secured! But did you know that this is one such habit that holds you back? Yes, it holds you back from achieving a lot many things that you have only dreamt of. When you stay in your own comfort zone, you will never know what you are capable of.

Hence, unless and until you try your hands on something and step out of your comfort zone, you will never know what you are truly capable of. Did you know that the brawny in the business, such as Bill Gates, Warren Buffet, and many other personalities, have all failed in life, at some point or the other! But what would have happened if they would have feared their failure and stayed in their comfort zone for the rest of their lives?

Remember, with the risk comes to the possibility of achieving a reward. Hence, why hold yourself back and stay in your comfort zone when you can explore, wander and try everything that comes your way to know what you are capable of! Imagine what a great learning experience it will be!

6. Waiting For The Right Moment

Do you really think that there is a right moment for everything? If there were, then the law of gravity would not have been discovered, neither would we have received more significant innovations in life. Well, it is up to you to choose a moment and act! Yes, it is as simple as that!
If you keep living your life wandering about the right moment that will control your life and that you have your own sweet time to do everything, you will only lose on your precious time. Instead, we all must be accountable for our actions each day and grab the opportunity to try, create, explore, invent, experiment, and a lot more!

7. The Image of Being Perfect

Don't we feel that everyone around us is living their perfect lives? Sorry to burst your bubble, it is not so! Thanks to social media, we are always misguided to believe that others live their fairytales while we are sulking in our own lives! This is when we keep pushing ourselves to live a perfect life, be a perfect person and make everyone around us perfect!
But is it practically possible to do so? In fact, with doing so, we tend to set an unrealistic expectation and tends to harm our mental well being and relationships around us. Life is about swinging in the right direction

at times, and sometimes in the opposite! Each of these scenarios brings with it its fruits, which must be graced with positivity.

Hence, let me tell you, there is no need for you to be perfect! Be however you are, but be your best version!

Conclusion:

Hence, kill these behaviors that hold you back. Instead, break the barrier and strive for a rewarding tomorrow. Let's try being a little different than we are? What say?

Chapter 32:
Happy People Are Optimistic

Beyond the simple reality that optimists are happier people (and happiness is what you're striving for), optimism has other benefits as well. So, if you want to achieve greater happiness, try being optimistic for a day.

Optimists enjoy a greater degree of academic success than pessimists do. Because optimistic students think it's possible for them to make a good grade, they study hardier and they study smarter. They manage the setting in which they study and they seek help from others when they need it. (Optimism, it turns out, is almost as predictive of how well students do in college as the SAT.)

Optimists are more self-confident than pessimists are. They believe in *themselves* more than fate.

Optimists are more likely to be problem-solvers than pessimists are. When pessimistic students get a D on a test, they tend to think things like: "I knew I shouldn't have taken this course. I'm no good at psychology." The optimistic student who gets a D says to herself, "I can do better. I just didn't study enough for this test. I'll do better next time." And she will.

Optimists welcome second chances after they fail more than pessimists do. Optimistic golfers always take a *mulligan* (a redo swing without penalty). Why? Because they expect to achieve a better result the second time around.

Optimists are more socially outgoing than pessimists are. Socially outgoing folks believe that the time they spend with other human beings makes them better in some way — smarter, more interesting, more attractive. Unfortunately, pessimists see little, if any, benefit from venturing out into the social world.

Optimists are not as lonely as pessimists are. Because pessimists don't see as much benefit from socializing with others, they have far fewer social and emotional connections in their lives, which is what loneliness is all about.

Optimists utilize social support more effectively than pessimists do. They aren't afraid to reach out in times of need.

Optimists are less likely to blame others for their misfortune than pessimists are. When you blame someone else for your troubles, what you're really saying is, "You're the *cause* of my problem and, therefore, you have to be the *solution* as well." Optimists have just as many troubles as pessimists throughout life — they just accept more responsibility for dealing with their misfortune.

Optimists cope with stress better than pessimists do. Pessimists worry, optimists act. A patient with coronary heart disease who is pessimistic "hopes and prays" that he doesn't have another heart attack anytime soon. The optimistic heart patient leaves little to chance — instead, he exercises regularly, practices his meditation exercises, adheres to a low-cholesterol diet, and makes sure he always gets a good night's sleep.

Chapter 33:
10 Habits of Prophet Muhammad

The Prophet Muhammad (peace be upon him) is a great man believed to have been a prophet of Allah. Born in Mecca about 570 in the common era (570 CE), the man who founded the Islam religion lived for sixty-two years, until he died in 632 CE.

Throughout his life, he was an inspiration to many people who believed in his calling. He lived an exemplary life and his followers emulated his habits. Here are ten habits of the prophet:

1. He Was A Man Of Unquestionable Integrity

The prophet led an honest life to the point even his staunchest enemies would vouch for him. Like other prophets in Islam; Ibrahim, Ismail, and Yusuf, prophet Muhammad was a truthful and very noble man.

At one time the prophet (peace be upon him) assembled all the Makkans in one place and asked them if they would believe him when he said that an army was approaching. Everybody said they will trust him because they have never heard him lie. The people believed him completely to trust him with their lives.

2. He Was Influential

Everywhere the prophet gave his speech, he managed to influence people to abandon their evil ways and draw closer to God. His speech rattled his enemies and they could not comprehend how he was able to command such a large following because his believers increased daily.

His influence, even in death, has not withered away. The world has at least 1.8 billion Muslims who believe in Islam and the doctrines that the prophet (peace be upon him) advanced.

3. **He Was Bold and Courageous**

Prophet Muhammad (peace be upon him) spoke fearlessly of God's message. He criticized rich merchants for their immorality and greed as they exploited the poor. He also spoke against ills in society with a call to action to reform.

Even when the prophet faced death threats, he remained firm in his resolve to fight injustice. His focus was to spread the message of Allah to the whole world.

4. **He Was Fair**

It can never be said that the Prophet (peace be upon him) has never been unfair throughout his documented life. He stood and championed for fairness regardless of who was right or wrong. His sole aim was to live the life of equity he was preaching.

There was once a dispute between a Jewish person who had been framed and a Muslim. He ruled in favor of the Jew after sufficient evidence was put before him. Were it not that he was fair, he could have sided with the Muslim.

5. **He Was Apt**

The prophet (peace be upon him) was fast and ready prepared for any eventuality. This made him the perfect leader. In him was a reliable person capable of representing them well.

He was an advocate of consulting. In his line of work, he would decide and act almost immediately. There was a time when he was preparing for a military expedition and a companion came to question him on the military plan. The prophet (peace be upon him) knew the different times of discussion and action. He did not allow himself to be distracted during such a crucial time.

6. **He Showed Servant Leadership**

Prophet Muhammad (peace be upon him) did not lead people to causes he did not believe in. He was at the forefront with his followers following behind. His words were laced with action and you could be sure he would abandon everything to attend to a bigger cause.

The prophet (peace be upon him) once said that the leader of a people is their servant. He did not believe in burdening his followers with his baggage. He served the people.

7. **He Was Patient**

The prophet (peace be upon him) was very patient to lengths that ordinary people could not attain. His patience was limitless and he did not complain when he passed through painful moments in his life.

In Ta'if, the people and their children stoned him until he was bleeding. He patiently endured the suffering while watching his followers being mistreated. It is his great patience that strengthened his followers to endure trials.

8. He Demonstrated Emotional Maturity

Prophet Muhammad (peace be upon him) was always positive despite prevailing difficult times. He insisted on self-happiness as well as that of other people. Even when it was expected that he would revenge on his enemies, the prophet showed emotional intelligence and forgave them.

The prophet taught that smiling was also a form of charity. This was not the face-value meaning of his statement. He was directing his followers to rise above petty squabbles and work towards positivity and emotional maturity just like him.

9. He Was Compassionate

Prophet Muhammad (peace be upon him) was compassionate to everyone. He did not hold grudges against his enemies. Instead, he would sympathize with their misfortunes and help them overcome them.

He once showed care and compassion by visiting an old woman who tormented him by throwing litter his way. The prophet (peace be upon him) helped her prepare food when she fell sick. He did not remember the ill she had done to him.

10. He Was A Peacemaker

Prophet Muhammad (peace be upon him) did not thrive in chaos and disorderliness. He was a peacemaker and intervened to calm a situation that could have turned chaotic. So understanding was he that he once stopped his followers from beating up a man who urinated in the mosque!

A Bedouin had come to a mosque of the prophet and urinated within the prayer area. The worshippers were angered and wanted to beat up the Bedouin. It is prophet Muhammad (peace be upon him) who intervened and defended the man.

He understood that it was a call of nature and the man could not stop himself. Were it not for the prophet's peace-keeping habit, the Bedouin could not survive the anger of the believers.

In conclusion, these are the ten pillar habits of prophet Muhammad (peace be upon him). They are dominant habits throughout his life.

Chapter 34:
10 Reasons Money Can't Buy You Happiness

I'm sure you have heard this statement before, that "Money can't buy happiness.", but have you stopped to think about why it might be so? Many of us chase money and that high paying job because we believe that it will bring us wealth which will in turn make us happy. We do it because it is what society tells us we should be doing. That we should trade all our time and energy to make money no matter how many sacrifices we have to make with regards to our friendships, relationships, and so on.

It is true that a certain income level and money in the bank is required to allow us to have a comfortable standard of living, which could make life quite nice for us. But beyond that, it will be tough to derive happiness from just sheer truckloads of money alone, as we will soon find out.

1. Our Happiness Is Not Derived From Material Things

This is arguably the most important yet easily overlooked aspect when it comes to dealing with money. While most of us will have desires to live in a dream home, owning the ultimate luxury car, and buying the greatest gifts we can buy when we're rich, we fail to realize that the process of acquisition of material things is a futile effort. It is always thrilling to be on the forefront of owning the latest material good on the market, but the excitement you have for a product usually fades away pretty quickly once you have them in your hands. We acclimatize very quickly to what we have, and we search for the next thing almost immediately. This seemingly endless chase for happiness would seem like a carrot on a stick, always dangling it's juiciness in front of you but you never get to taste it. If you look around at the things you have in your house, you will know what I mean. All the stuff that was once intriguing to you now no longer has the same effect of joy and happiness that it once had. Bottom line is that there is no amount of stuff you can acquire that will ever make you truly happy.

2. Money Cannot Buy You Relationships

We fail to realize the power of relationships when it comes to the happiness equation. Happiness can easily be derived from thriving relationships. Relationships that serve to enrich our lives in all aspects of it. When we are in a relationship with someone who loves and cares for us unconditionally, there is no amount of money that can buy you that feeling. The same goes for friendships and family. Having people that support you in your endeavors, grieve with you when you experience loss, or just someone you can talk to, to share your feelings of excitement, sorrow, and all the different ranges of emotions, those are the moments that truly matter in life.

3. Money Could Lure Disingenuous People

While some may argue that you can buy friendships by paying people to be around you, I am pretty sure most of you wouldn't want to go down that path. You know that these people are not hanging around you because they like you, but because they like what you have in your pocket. Genuine relationships are ones that will last even when you don't have a dime left in your back account. When all else fails, you will want to have these people around you for support.

4. You Will Never Feel Like You have Enough Money

Chasing money as a substitute for happiness is a tricky thing. We all think we need $1 million dollars in our bank account to be happy, but as soon as we hit that milestone, something just doesn't feel quite right. We feel empty inside, we feel like maybe it's not enough, so we set a bigger target of $2 million. But that day will come too and again we will feel like something is amiss. The cycle repeats itself until we finally realize that deriving happiness from a monetary goal is also a futile effort.

5. Money Only Helps To Improve Your Standard of Living

Instead of using money as bait for happiness, use it for what it really is for - survival, food, clothing, a roof over your head, and the occasional splurge on something you like. Beyond that, look elsewhere for happiness. I am here to tell you that it is human nature for us to feel like we never have enough of something, and that includes money. We have been programmed to always want and need more. More of everything. We compare to people more successful than us and think we need to live like them in order to be happy. Don't make the same mistake as everyone else. Find a comfortable amount you need for survival and retirement, and the rest is bonus.

6. Making Money Requires Sacrifices

Unless you're a trust fund baby, or money falls from the sky, or you managed to strike a jackpot, constantly putting money above all else requires time and effort to earn. Working 12 hour shifts, 7 days a week is no easy feat. You will see your youth fly by and your other priorities fall by the wayside. By the time you've earned the desired income of your dreams, you may well find that a few decades have passed and you're standing on top of the mountain, alone, with no one to share that experience with. No one who may be able to travel with you or even spend that money with you. Unless you consciously try for a balanced work-life, you will find it quite a lonesome experience.

7. The Simple Pleasures In Life Doesn't Require That Much Money

Spending time with your family, going out for coffee with friends, having a chill board games night on the weekends with enthusiasts like yourself, you will find that all these activities brings us closer to the emotional world. The emotional and spiritual connection we have with fellow human beings that bring us laughter, joy, sadness, and happiness. We fail to realize that the happiest moments we can create doesn't require that much money. It just requires planning and some food. Stop chasing the dream vacation halfway around the world for happiness. It is underneath you all along.

8. You Lack the Happiness Mindset

Happiness is merely a feeling, and feelings can be created by choice. Money can't fix your emotional problems, it can only buy you therapy. Ultimately, it's your attitude and mindset that determines your level of happiness that you experience. If you always see the glass half empty, no amount of money can make you see the glass as half full.

9. You Don't Feel Grateful for The Things Money Buy You

We take for granted the things we have acquired so far and only look towards the next shiny object. Being grateful for our hard-earned money has bought us thus far should be our number one priority. Treasure the bed you bought that you can sleep comfortably in, be thankful for the television you have that allows you to stream your favourite shows on demand, be grateful for the roof that houses all these items and protects you from the elements.

10. We Fall into The If-Then Trap of Chasing Money

How many times do you have the thought that the next promotion you receive will be the happiest moment of your life. Or perhaps that your boss will give me a raise if you turn this project in successfully. If we only chase our paychecks rather than chase fulfillment, we are running the wrong race in life.

Remember these important points the next time you work for money. Yes, having money is important, but it should not adversely affect your ability to live a fulfilling life. There are a million other things that are just as equally important if you're chasing happiness.

www.ingramcontent.com/pod-product-compliance
Lightning Source LLC
Chambersburg PA
CBHW070918080526
44589CB00013B/1355